CORPORATE ESCAPE

THE RISE OF THE NEW ENTREPRENEUR

Dear Maxine,

To a life full of Purpose & Fulfillment.

Enjoy the reading!

Maité

CORPORATE ESCAPE

THE RISE OF THE NEW ENTREPRENEUR

MAITE BARÓN

Corporate Escape
The Rise Of The New Entrepreneur

First published in 2012 by

Ecademy Press

48 St Vincent Drive, St Albans, Herts, AL1 5SJ

info@ecademy-press.com

www.ecademy-press.com

Cover design by Maite Barón & Kiryl Lysenka

Interior design by Julie Oakley

Printed on acid-free paper from managed forests. This book is printed on demand, so no copies will be remaindered or pulped.

ISBN 978-1-908746-40-5

The right of Maite Barón to be identified as the author of this work has been inserted in accordance with sections 77 and 78 of the Copyright Designs and Patents Act 1988.

A CIP catalogue record for this book is available from the British Library.

All rights reserved. No part of this book may be reproduced in any material form (including photocopying or storing in any medium by electronic means and whether or not transiently or incidentally to some other use of this publication) without the written permission of the copyright holder except in accordance with the provisions of the Copyright, Design and Patents Act 1988. Applications for the Copyright holders written permission to reproduce any part of this publication should be addressed to the publishers.

This book is available online and at all good bookstores.

© 2012 Maite Barón

Dedication

I dedicate this book to Keith...

...and to the people who have the courage to live their lives with passion.

To those who fight the odds for what they believe, becoming who they were born to become. To those who use their power, influence, means and determination to raise the standards of human excellence.

To those who are not scared to stand up for others in the pursuit of justice, and those who raise human awareness and consciousness about people, nature, our planet and the world as *one* intertwined and interconnected community that transcends nations and frontiers.

I humbly dedicate this book to the soul gardeners who care and believe in people's potential. To all of you who are committed to make the world a better place by leaving a legacy where humanity is at the core.

I hope that the ideas in this book will assist and inspire you into action, because what you do matters.

> *"Act always as if the future of the universe depends on everything you do, while laughing at yourself for thinking that anything you do makes any difference whatsoever."*
>
> — Buddhist teaching

Table Of Contents

Acknowledgements	ix
Introduction	1

Part I: Prosperity — 7

Chapter 1 – Walking In Between Two Worlds	9
Chapter 2 – What A Mess	31
Chapter 3 – Reality Doesn't Exist... Really	55
Chapter 4 – Life Is About Choices	83

Part II: Purpose — 117

Chapter 5 – Change Is Difficult Until You Know Why And How	119
Chapter 6 – There Is Nothing To Be Afraid Of, Take Off And Learn To Fly	151
Chapter 7 – Today Is The First Day Of The Rest Of Your Life To Start Afresh	171
Conclusion	199
Afterword	203
Don't Forget To Get Your Bonuses: Next Steps	207
About The Author	209

Acknowledgements

Thank you...

To Keith: The ONE who brings the best out of me day by day and who makes my heart and soul sing. Without you this book would never have come into the world. Thank you for your love, support and believing in me. Above all, thank you for being YOU.

> *"Follow your bliss and the universe will open doors where there were only walls."*
>
> *Joseph Campbell*

To my parents: who now live between the sun, the moon and the stars. Thank you for showing me the world and the beauty of different cultures, for raising me with passion, humility and fairness and for helping me to see people for who they are. Also for the amazing experiences we lived and shared together. I would not be who I am today without you.

> *"Even after all this time, the Sun never says to the Earth, you owe me. Look what happens with a love like that, it lights the whole sky."*
>
> *Hafiz*

To my mentors: Robert Dilts and Stephen Gilligan who taught me how to see beyond.

> *"The ageless melody, unheard, heals;*
> *the healing vision, unseen, leads; the*
> *true leaders, immortal, know..."*
>
> *Kahlil Gibran*

To all of you who have supported me during the creation of this book, directly or indirectly.

Introduction

Welcome!

If you're reading this book then you're probably an experienced professional, executive or manager who is already realising that many aspects of your life cannot carry on as they are, and yet you can't see a way forward, or are feeling confused about your options.

Perhaps you are even going through a period of significant change that is, quite naturally, making you feel rather scared and overwhelmed.

In this you are not alone...

A growing number of professionals are finding themselves in the same situation, and now, like you, are seeking deeper answers about their way forward.

This book is your first step towards making important (some might say radical) changes in your life that will not only answer the questions that you may be having, but also and more importantly, inspire you to take action and move ahead... before it's too late.

Some of what you will learn here may challenge your preconceptions – I make no apologies because that's what it's meant to do!

My goal is to open your mind to new possibilities, to expand your thinking and help you confront the social paradigms that are keeping you stuck in a rut, and which got you here in the first place. The old and familiar answers will not support you in becoming emotionally resilient in a way that will help you face and overcome the real world challenges that lie ahead.

> *I'm not here to tell you what is true for you or not. What I'm doing is giving you a chance to look at your life from a different perspective, to look at your current reality as an objective observer to see the level of truth for yourself. And then, for YOU to decide what do you want to do about it*

The words above define what this book is about – helping professionals like you take control of their lives so they can leave uncertainty, confusion and fear behind.

If you are one of those whose working life is far removed from what you once dreamed of, if you are feeling stuck, frustrated, unvalued, burned out or just not reaching your potential, then this book will help you to see what is going on. It will open your eyes so you realise that you already have all the resources you need to create the changes you want to make, if you choose to do something about it.

This book has a special place in my heart for those professionals who are in transition and looking for new answers about what to do next. This includes those wanting to escape the corporate world, those between jobs or in between careers, those frustrated by unsuccessful job hunting because they are still selecting vacancies on the basis of conformity rather than their own personal passions and interests.

This book is also relevant to people who may be questioning some of their personal relationships, not just marriages or intimate relationships, but their connections with parents, friends or colleagues, which they are now finding draining rather than uplifting.

Finally, this book is for those professionals who want to start and grow their own business, those whom I call the New Entrepreneurs.

INTRODUCTION

Right now, no matter which category you fit into, you all have one thing in common and that is that you want to escape from one thing into something better as you are all professionals in transition.

My mission is to help you wake up and to shift your mindset, to make you understand that you don't need to sell your soul for money, that there are other alternatives available to you, and that you are much more resourceful than you give yourself credit for.

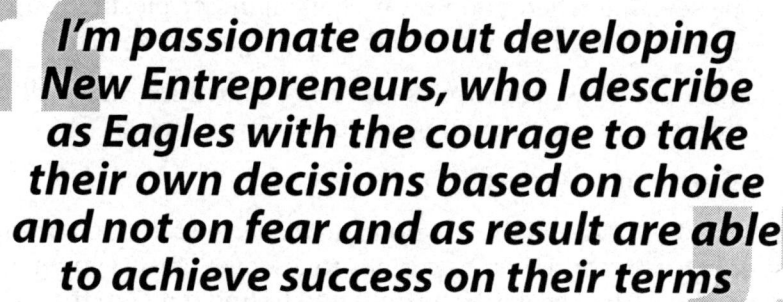

I'm passionate about developing New Entrepreneurs, who I describe as Eagles with the courage to take their own decisions based on choice and not on fear and as result are able to achieve success on their terms

WARNING: This book contains powerful ideas

Behind the obvious theme of this book, which is based on the seven steps of my Corporate Escape System™, there is a hidden theme, a 'story behind the story', and it's that which actually matters most, as you will discover, but only when you are ready to see it and act upon it.

For those who just like to read book after book, as though browsing through pictures in a travel brochure but with no intention of taking the trip, you may find the content challenging and might even finish the book without ever discovering its real inner message, but I hope that this is not you.

However, just to give you a clue, when it becomes obvious to you, you will feel a powerful sensation in your body, your mind will start thinking bigger as a new vision for your life will expand in front of you and you will feel resourceful and strong. You will know you can make it happen no matter what. You will feel in full control of your life and your destiny and a desire to take charge.

With each chapter you will feel closer to discovering that hidden message. The chapters are set in a particular order for a reason. So, the first time you read the book it's best to read the chapters in sequence, but re-read them at random, if you wish, just going back to the pages that call to you again and again.

For some of you, it may take you the whole book to find the hidden message, for others it will never happen.

It's up to you how you read the book, reading it through from beginning to end, persevering when you find it challenging or picking it up and putting it down every time something you read upsets you.

As I mentioned before, sometimes I will say something that will push your buttons, and then you will be faced with two choices:

Get upset about it and give up, or,

Notice what has triggered the reaction and made you feel uncomfortable, angry, or frustrated and then be curious to discover what is going on under the surface. Go deeper, it's the only way to find out. Yes, that takes a bit of effort, but it is worth it because the lessons you learn will be useful for the rest of your life and so will be a good return on your investment.

Trust me... everything you're about to read is born of personal experience, not abstract theory or new age mumbo jumbo. I have experienced periods of change several times throughout my life, sometimes through choice, sometimes not, so everything you read here is based on methods and techniques that have worked wonders in my own life and in those of my clients. So, I invite you to be curious and open to exploring the exercises and activities I suggest. I can't guarantee they will work for you, but I know they will help you move forward in your own way for sure and wherever you happen to be right now.

Now get a pen, you will need it, or better still download your own Resources Pack from **www.maitebaron.com/resourcepack** in which you will find more bonus exercises to help you move forward.

A life filled with passion, purpose and prosperity starts here!

INTRODUCTION

Let Me Start By Telling You The Tale of An Eagle

The Eagle can live for 70 years. But to reach this age, on about its 40th birthday the Eagle must make a hard decision, whether to die soon or whether to go through a painful process of CHANGE.

It must do this because it has reached a point in its life when its once long and flexible talons can no longer grab prey and the sharp beak of its younger years has become ever more bent. Even its wings are now too heavy with matted feathers, making it more difficult to fly.

If the Eagle chooses to do nothing it will die, but to change it must fly to a mountain top and knock its beak against the hard rock until it breaks off. It also needs to pluck out its talons and feathers then wait until new ones to grow back so it is able to take its famous flight of rebirth and live for another thirty years or more.

And why does the Eagle need to change at all?

So that it can survive and thrive.

You too have to start a process of change... sometimes this means getting rid of fixed mindsets, negative habits, social conditioning, unpleasant memories, or letting go of past relationships and taking decisions based on your new values. But only by freeing yourself from past burdens can you take advantage of present opportunities.

So, to create the life *you* want, you need to fly high again and soar like an Eagle...!

Part I

Prosperity

"God created all men equal. Why do some accomplish far greater accomplishments than others? Because they had a vision, a desire, and they took action."

Thomas J. Vilord

Chapter 1

Walking In Between Two Worlds

The Old World Is Collapsing And New Parameters Are Being Created

Today you are walking in between two worlds and the old working paradigms and what used to be the safest option are now your biggest threat.

When you grew up you were made to believe that going to university, studying hard and getting a degree or diploma will get you sorted for life. You found your first job and maybe had a few more during your working life. Perhaps you were expecting this situation to carry on till the day you retired. However, now you're starting to realise that this is not going to be the case…

Organisations have become more powerful than governments and so omnipotent that it was unthinkable they could fail; however they are failing, and no doubt more is to come.

Current events may have already turned your world upside down, making the impossible real and the possible doubtful. Nothing seems real anymore.

Well maybe it was, after all you only see the world as a reflection of who you are, or to put it another way, you only ever perceive a distorted reality, the one you choose to see.

But now you need to create new parameters and shift the perspective of your professional life. Unfortunately, when you were growing up nobody told you that you were in charge of your destiny and that you could become whoever you wanted to become and that you could use your own inner wisdom and guidance to help you find your way forward.

Can you ever remember having this type of conversation with your parents, teachers, siblings, friends, or even reading such ideas in any newspaper, book or magazine? Has anyone ever told you this? Probably not.

What you heard back then was very different, and it was this that shaped your map of the world and your expectations, and so determined how your life has turned out, at least until today.

You did what you were told, you worked, and perhaps are still working, for a large organisation, with others taking the key decisions about your life, not you. You can only hope that these organisations do well and carry on growing their profits because they hold your destiny in their hands. As you did what you were told, you haven't developed your own decision-making powers, well perhaps you have for the little things, but not for what really matters, taking ownership of your life.

You studied what was required to get your foot in the door, and you are doing what is expected of you. At the end of the day you are tired and you seldom use your free time to update your skills. You have been thinking about it for a while, even asked for a couple of prospectuses online, but being unsure of your options you have decided to postpone this important decision for later, as there is always time.

So here you are today, with a set of skills that are more and more easily outsourced or replaced, a generalist lost in a cloud of international talent, left waiting to see if they are writing your name on the wall, and knowing that unless you do something about it, it's only a matter of time before they do so.

I don't want to scare you, but I know this is an uncomfortable truth, the one you don't want to hear, the silent one that has been keeping thousands of professionals sleepless for a while.

> **It's time to wake up from a sleep-walking trance that is putting your life on hold #CorporateEscape**

But most professionals still wait until decisions are made for them. In other words, until they are made redundant, or when options disappear altogether.

Unfortunately by then, valuable time has been wasted, their skills are often rusty and they feel trapped in a circle that just keeps going round until it breaks.

The wake-up call is never nice, unless of course, you are prepared.

The reason why most professionals live a life of unfulfilled frustration is because they become used to living with a great level of discomfort. Each day they kid themselves that everybody else is feeling the same way too. After all, isn't this the way life is supposed to turn out when you become a responsible adult?

So, they prefer to carry on like this, playing small, suffering, giving up their dreams and hopes rather than facing the truth. Because when you acknowledge what is really going on in your life, you know that the level of pain and despair you are feeling is only going to get worse.

And though you want to avoid any change as much as possible, you already know that ultimately you will need to do something about it. You can't keep running away from your truth forever, just waiting for your real life to start some day.

You need to get ready and change like the Eagle in the story or you will perish and disappear as professional opportunities that could have been yours go to someone else who is better prepared and willing to take the risks.

At any given time, you have choices available to you and it is the quality of your decisions that will determine the quality of your life as a whole, in every area of your life, with no exceptions.

You Are In Charge Of Your Destiny

It's unrealistic to depend on someone else to manage your life. Being an adult means far more than adding years to your passport, it means that you are the one who has to take conscious control of your own life.

But, believe it or not, many adults prefer to allow others to make the important decisions in their lives for them. Often they don't do this consciously or explicitly, but as a result of inaction.

Childhood is based on dependency (others providing for you), but adulthood should be based on independence (being able to cope emotionally with your life events and providing for yourself) as well as in *inter*dependency (contributing to the lives of others).

So, being an adult in the full sense of the word implies personal responsibility. But that is the one thing that so many wish to ignore. Yet you are the one who is really responsible for your health, for your body, for the state of your mind, for keeping fit, for being active and for being employable and financially independent.

But many will leave this responsibility to others, and instead concentrate on wanting and having more – more money to go on holidays, to buy a newer or better computer, or to get the latest gadgets.

Often they compare themselves with others; not so much looking at what others are doing to earn more, but simply feeling resentful and asking themselves 'Why am I not paid more?' So, they want the rewards but without the effort, something that is not possible any more.

And, now a moment of truth is facing you. Let me explain what I mean with this story.

The Barber And The King

The Barber was giving a haircut to the King and as all barbers do, he began a conversation with his regal customer.

'Your Majesty', he said, 'I have been wondering why it is that the King's Minister is paid so very much more than myself. This seems unfair. Why does he deserve this and I do not?'

The King thought for a moment and then said: 'So that you may see, I will give you a task to perform that I would normally give to my Minister. When you have done this, you will be able to judge this matter for yourself. Now, go down to the harbour and see if a ship has recently arrived and then come back and tell me about it.'

Excitedly, the Barber ran down to the harbour, found that a ship had recently arrived, then ran back to the King with his new found knowledge.

'I have found that a ship has newly docked,' said the Barber to the King.

'And when did it arrive?' asked the King.

The barber thought for a moment, then turned on his heel and ran back down to the harbour, before shortly returning.

'Two days ago,' said the Barber to the King.

'And what cargo is it carrying?' asked the King.

The Barber set off again, and returned.

'Spices,' said the Barber rather breathlessly.

'And where has it come from?' asked the King.

The Barber set off again and after slightly longer returned with more new found knowledge.

'The Far East,' said by now a very tired Barber.

'Thank you,' said the King, 'and now I think it is time you took a rest while my Minister has a go.'

The King called to his Minister and gave him the same task.

Soon the Minister was back and able to answer all the King's questions without having to make another trip to the harbour.

'And that is why,' said the King turning to the Barber, 'he is paid more than you!'

And the moral of this story?

Don't compare yourself with others. Everyone has their own strengths and weaknesses. Instead, work on your strengths and not your weaknesses, and always try to learn from those who are ahead of you.

Let's get another insight.

Throughout this book you will find exercises like the one below that will help you move forward with your life. If you read the whole book from cover to cover **and** do all these exercises, I can guarantee you that you will be much further ahead than most of the professionals around you, although a book can never truly replace the chemistry that comes from working with a coach.

Alternatively, attend one of our programmes like **The Corporate Escape Accelerated Programme: 7 Steps To Become A New Entrepreneur**™, which will give you a real competitive advantage when it comes to creating the life you want.

But don't just take my word, see for yourself by working through the book. Remember, you can download a Resources Pack that will help you from **www.maitebaron.com/resourcepack**

> **Exercise 1**
> 1. What are your beliefs about success (whatever that success means to you)?
> 2. Why do you think others are more successful than you?
> 3. How do you feel when you are around successful and wealthy people? Frustrated and resentful? Or do they inspire you to achieve more for yourself?
> 4. In what ways do you compare yourself to others? Where do you focus your attention? What things do you notice, and what things do you ignore?
> 5. What would you like to do differently so that you get the most from your skills and talents?

Your Notes

....

....

....

....

....

The Brave World Of The New Entrepreneurs Is Waiting For You To Join

There is no such thing any more as a job or career for life, so many professionals are now having to look for new answers.

And that means, irrespective of your current situation, it is essential to have a plan B, because in all likelihood, plan B will become your plan A overnight.

Today, professionals who find themselves between jobs, or between careers, and those who are being made redundant realise that their only remaining option is to become an entrepreneur. This is not so much by desire or choice, but rather as a result of circumstance, either because they haven't had success with the more usual options, or because what is actually available doesn't feel right anymore, or because they now want different things from their working life.

I call this group of professionals the New Entrepreneurs.

Being an entrepreneur, whether New or traditional, is as much about having distinctive attitudes, beliefs, mindset, as it is knowing about business, finance or being marketing savvy.

And, acquiring these attitudes, beliefs and mindsets is the first and possibly most important step to becoming a successful entrepreneur since you need to start thinking in the right way long before you begin to tackle more practical issues. If you don't shift your mindset the rest will not compensate for this, leading often, I'm sorry to say, to failure.

And failure is what this book will help you avoid, by guiding you on a path that takes you from where you are to where you want to be, by teaching you to think and behave like a New Entrepreneur.

All entrepreneurs are in one way or another nonconformists who view the world in a very different way to the vast majority. They see opportunities where others only see problems.

Often traditional entrepreneurs have grown up this way, either as a result of family influences, or because of some other aspect of their early lives. New Entrepreneurs, however, are those who discover their nonconformity later in life, often doing so through frustration and unfulfilled experiences.

Everyone, including you, has a nonconformist inside themselves that's being suppressed by the limiting world you live in.

But now is the right time for breaking free and joining the *New Entrepreneurs*.

You, like everyone, have baggage that restricts your current choices and chances of success, and unless you get the right support and put in the required effort this is not going to change.

Your current mindset, your existing beliefs, your everyday habits, your routines and your paradigms have brought you to where you are today. These need to be updated, because they will not get you to the destination you want to reach. Of course, change always requires effort and endurance, which is why it's crucial that you have the support you need to build the resilience needed to succeed in your quest!

So, let's examine what I see day in, day out, working with professionals in states of change, people like you, in search of a new professional direction, or a new meaning for the work they do, as they leave old style employment for the world of the New Entrepreneur.

Some of the following descriptions may not fully apply to you, others will, but look beyond the surface of each and notice what strikes a chord because only by acknowledging your own reality can you really create something different.

> **What matters most is to notice the trends & patterns that distinguish an employee mindset from that of the New Entrepreneur #CorporateEscape** 🐦

Characteristics	Old Style Employee Mindset	New Entrepreneur's Mindset
Identity	I'm an employee	I'm a New Entrepreneur
Beliefs Capital	I have no control over external events	The world is my oyster
World view	Others will make it happen for me	I'm responsible for my own success
	'I'm not good enough'	'I'm good enough and I will carry on learning from others who are better than me'
Working preference	I would always prefer and want to work for someone else	I want to work for myself and to start my own business
	I would only work for myself if there is no other choice	Or to team up with like-minded people to create something new
Emotional Capital	I can become quickly discouraged because I haven't developed the *resilience muscle* that I need	I turn problems into opportunities and setbacks into experiences. I always want to learn so that *next time I will know better*
Emotional Intelligence	I want quick results	
Emotional Resilience	A setback can last me a lifetime, and I will often think about giving up altogether	I am willing to do what it takes to overcome the odds

Characteristics	Old Style Employee Mindset	New Entrepreneur's Mindset
Motivational Capital	I'm motivated best by others and am used to being told what to do	I'm a self starter and self-motivated. I decide what to do and what the priorities are
	I'm ambitious. I want more to have more to spend	I'm ambitious. I want more so I can create something else that's bigger and better
	I prefer to avoid as much risk as possible so I generally look at what I may lose instead of what I could win	I am willing to take risks for the things I want
	I tend to move *away from* things because I'm fearful of the consequences	I prefer to move *towards* things and love being rewarded for doing so
Personal Responsibility	If I feel a little bit under the weather I will normally call in sick	I don't have time to be sick and I take responsibility for my own health
		My business needs me so I need to keep fit, because I know I'm responsible for my own success
Relational Capital	I need to 'fit' in with everyone else so I try to 'conform', to be 'accepted'	I have close groups of friends, and relatives. I use social media purposefully
	I'm used to working with others and often find it difficult to work on my own for long periods	I believe in personal recommendations. I mostly have one-to-one relationships and am good at creating partnerships
		I can work alone or with teams

Characteristics	Old Style Employee Mindset	New Entrepreneur's Mindset
Money Capital	I'm going to be paid a salary, so it's better I choose a profession or job that pays as much as possible	I'm responsible for my own success, so the more I put in, the more I will get out
Money Beliefs	Even if I were to start my own business I'd probably still behave like an employee instead of a business owner	My background is not so important, what matters is what I want to create
	I don't know how to make this identity shift	I believe I deserve to be successful and I will *be*
Money Behaviours	I like to **spend**. The main reason to have a job is so I'm able to pay the bills and then have money to spend on holidays, cars, entertainment	I like to **invest** in myself and my education and I want to see return on that investment
	Saving is not a priority so it mostly doesn't happen	I understand the importance of **saving** and investing
	I'm always spending on 'perishable things' instead of investing for long term returns (i.e. buying plenty of cheap clothes instead of just one quality suit)	Quality is more important to me than quantity
	I choose poor role models and often spend money that I don't have trying to be like them	I **invest** my money on what matters to me and in my business
	I lack planning skills and don't understand about money dynamics and wealth creation	

Characteristics	Old Style Employee Mindset	New Entrepreneur's Mindset
Business Savvy Capital	I have very little, if any, understanding of business models and systems or basic knowledge of how money, numbers or business work	I grew up wanting to have my own business, and am always looking to learn about business from others Or I grew up in the family business
Time preference Capital	I'm very focused on the present and want immediate gratification	Present: I need to put in whatever effort it takes right now to make things happen. I'm an action taker Future: I'm willing to give time to the things that will give me a return on my investment
Business Based On	I don't want to have or run a business, I just want a job	The Traditional Entrepreneur: I need large sums of capital, and infrastructure for my business The New Entrepreneur: My business is based on ideas, knowledge and expertise. I focus on leveraging my intellectual property and create assets
Financial Business Needs	I don't think about this at all. I don't even care or understand what the business owner has to go through to pay me, just so long as I get my salary I'm happy	The Traditional Entrepreneur: I need a large upfront investment to get things going The New Entrepreneur: I can start a business with just an idea, a computer and creating strategic partnerships

Characteristics	Old Style Employee Mindset	New Entrepreneur's Mindset
How business finances are obtained	N/A	The Traditional Entrepreneur: I find funds through personal relationships, banks, family and friends
		The New Entrepreneur: I find funds through personal relationships, family and friends as well as attracting investment angels, venture capitalists and crowd funding for my ideas through social media and word of mouth
		I think money travels fast to ideas that are worth investing in!

Understandably, if you have worked most of your professional life for somebody else, your business knowledge is probably limited. Until now you have replicated the same working patterns that you saw when you were growing up. This has been your map of the world so far.

Having worked for someone else for so long has also made a dent in your mindset, leading you to instinctively follow the crowd, rather than standing up for yourself, and to favour the safest option. You still operate from this mindset: 'someone else is going to sort things out for me'.

From your standpoint the solution is always perceived as coming from the outside world, whether that's a large employer, the government or some other institution.

This isn't surprising when we are all so used to the 'nanny state' heritage we have all been part of, either as active participants or as perplexed witnesses.

But this can't go on, if you want to succeed.

Your perception of money is also coloured by your upbringing, your social paradigms and the environment in which you grew up and you are living in. This means that most adults don't believe that abundance is a birthright or available to them. So, they just work to pay their bills and believe that the minimum is the norm. You see wealth as something only available to those few who are lucky, or greedy, or nasty, or in some way very different from you.

But whatever beliefs about money and wealth you currently hold, they are the result of the social conditioning you have absorbed. The good news is that you can update your limiting beliefs at any time and this book will show you how to create healthy money beliefs as well as a clear purpose, a vision for your life and values to guide you through so that you can finally take control of every area of your life.

So, let's start to make that happen.

The Four Seasons

A father with four sons wanted them to learn not to judge situations and others too quickly so he sent each in turn on a quest to look at a pear tree a great distance away.

The first son went in the winter, the second in spring, the third in summer, and the youngest in the autumn.

When all had returned, the father called them together so they could tell him what they had seen.

The first son said that the tree was ugly, bent and twisted.

The second said, 'No, the tree was covered with green buds and was full of promise.'

The third son thought differently again and described how it was laden with beautiful blossoms and smelled so sweet. It was the most graceful thing he had ever seen.

The last son disagreed with them all, saying that the tree was drooping under the weight of its fruit, and was full of life and fulfillment.

The father then explained to his sons that they were all right, because each had seen only one season in the tree's life.

So, he explained that you cannot judge a tree, or a person, by just one season, and that the essence of who we are and the pleasure, joy, and love that comes from life can only be measured at the end, when all the seasons are seen.

And the moral of this story?

If you give up when it's winter, you will miss the promise of your spring, the beauty of your summer and the fulfillment of your autumn.

So, don't let the pain of one cold season destroy the joy of all the rest. Persevere through the difficult patches and better times are sure to come. Resilience is the key.

Exercise 2

1. In which season are you professionally, right now?
2. In which season are you personally, right now?
3. What other seasons have you experienced professionally?
4. What other seasons have you experienced personally?
5. What seasons have you experienced with money?
6. How open are you to explore other seasons in different areas of your life, by doing and thinking differently?

Your Notes

You may think that I'm being a bit hard, judgmental or not being empathetic for not understanding your situation and all the struggles you are facing today.

Believe me I do, which is why I want to help you to wake up from the trance that you are in.

There is an important difference between empathy and sympathy. The first is about understanding how you feel, what you are going through and then allowing you to find your own solutions, so next time you can handle things differently.

Sympathy, on the other hand, is for people who want someone else to find the solution for them, or better still, to clear up the mess they have managed to create for themselves.

Unfortunately, there is too much sympathy around. This means that many people rely on someone else to manage their lives and make important decisions for them, a situation that will perpetuate until those involved learn how to find solutions to their problems for themselves.

My grandfather started the family business after the Spanish Civil War, and because things were hard, it paid my father only a minimum salary, not just to control costs, but so he would also understand the value of money. So, my parents respected money and I grew up believing that you can't spend what you don't have.

As a child I was told and encouraged to save for a 'rainy day'. When I started work as an employee I kept any little amounts I could, understanding that the amount was less important than developing the habit. When I was made redundant at 28 I knew that my modest savings would come in handy.

Consequently, all my life I have made sure I had no debts and worked hard for what I have achieved. When I started my business after being made redundant, I invested everything I had in it, sometimes having barely enough left to buy a sandwich in the supermarket until a client bought something from me. Living in a foreign country with few friends and no family around didn't make it any easier.

Those were hard times, but I felt in control of my life, knowing that it was only a matter of time until I would get some return even though I was not sure what this would be. But I truly believed in what I was doing and had full commitment and passion. Sometimes there were moments of frustration, fear and desperation when of course I wanted to quit, but these lasted only until I woke the next day and felt strong again to carry on with the vision of what I wanted to create back fresh in my mind.

I always wanted to be my own boss and to have my own business so I could be fully in charge of my destiny. Even though my first business was not very successful, I still got a return on my investment in so many ways, because I learned from my experiences.

I've been creating the life I wanted for the last fourteen years, always updating my vision and aligning it with my values so as to achieve success on my terms, with integrity and in a way that would allow me to leave behind a worthwhile legacy to the world.

So I understand where you are and I'm not saying that the journey you have to take will be quick and easy, as so many gurus want you to believe, although of course good things can happen quickly, especially in a fast-moving business environment.

Fortunately, today you have opportunities that were not available even a decade ago, and which mean you can become a New Entrepreneur with the minimum of investment and barely more than an idea and a computer. Not so long ago this was impossible, with most businesses requiring a large capital investment in production facilities and infrastructure.

Today factories can deliver small production runs of anything you want from computer covers and handbags through to Indian sauces, which means you can also test the market cost-effectively and in a way that once could only have been done by big business.

Technology has also made it possible to reach thousands of people in a matter of no time at all when before you would have needed to have an enormous PR and advertising budget to do the same. Now, you can even have your own TV channel 24/7 on YouTube and other platforms. Computers are affordable and you can use them to work from anywhere without needing an office. What's more, business hubs can give you access to all the office equipment and meeting space you need for just a small fee.

Today local also means global.

As you can see, there are plenty of advantages for the New Entrepreneur, though only if you make the necessary shift in mindset first to reset your current world view, beliefs, routines, habits and paradigms so you can succeed in our brave new world.

However, while I see many professionals who are trying to change direction by starting their own business and taking control of their lives, many still continue to fail, barely able to make ends meet because they are still held hostage by their old ways of thinking.

In effect, they are walking in a new world but with their old mindset, with an old image of themselves as someone who is still employed. As a result they behave like employees in their own business and guess what, yes... like this they won't ever succeed!

You may be thinking by now: 'I understand that I need an update, but this is not easy, otherwise everybody would be doing it.'

Exactly! And this is the main difference between the traditional and the New Entrepreneur who does things not because they are easy but because they are important and matter to them. This is the mindset you need to develop.

Sadly, it is not because they didn't have enough clients or sufficient money to invest that most new businesses fail, but because of the owner's mindset. And this is my point, with the right mindset you **will** find a way to get more clients and finances for your business. You will also know when to ask for help and understand the importance of prioritising and timing.

> **Most business owners run a Frankenstein business where they are the centre of a non universe. Everything revolves around them, so they are the CEOE, Chief Executives Of Everything which is the perfect vehicle for going nowhere apart from burn out and out of business**

Wherever you are coming from is less important than knowing where you are going to, what you want to achieve and why this is important to you.

There will always be poor and rich people, but you need to choose which side you want to be on and it's your money mindset more than anything else that will determine this. Your limiting beliefs about money will keep you from the success you could have, not because you lack skills, knowledge and expertise but because you don't know how to leverage them to your advantage.

What many professionals seem to miss is that unless you have money you can't make much difference to others because you can't give them what you don't have. By saying this, I don't mean that you need a lot of money to start your own business, but that you need to be paid properly for the services and expertise you offer. If you have limiting beliefs about money you will not charge what you are worth, and I see this often.

During my work with professionals we look at money beliefs and habits in depth to discover the blockages, a very liberating experience when you can untangle the mystery that keeps you trapped. But, we will look more at beliefs later, for now just remember that today in the world of the New Entrepreneur, you can have fulfillment from doing something that you love, and abundance at the same time.

> *So, make a choice, get ready to learn how to survive and thrive in this new world and ask for help when you need it. To have the right support is also key*

You Are Given A Second Chance To Survive And Thrive

There are four intertwined themes you will find running through this book.

Theme 1: The Rise Of The New Entrepreneur

I have already introduced you to the Eagles – the professionals who have or develop the courage to turn challenges into opportunities so they can take control of their lives and create their realities. Now it is time to introduce you to the Chickens – those who live in fear, depending on others, never wanting to take responsibility for their own life and success or failure.

Theme 2: The Link Between Leadership And Love

I refer to Leadership here not in the traditional sense – you will notice that it is written with a capital 'L' – but in the sense of Self-Leadership, an aspect that is often overlooked because it's easier to try to lead others than to lead yourself through life. However, unless you can do this, nothing else will feel right for you. So, I truly believe that without an open heart, without doing something you love with commitment and passion, and without healthy relationships in all areas of your life (both personal and professional), you will never feel free and in charge of your own destiny. Instead, you will be unfulfilled no matter what you do, how you do it, or how much you are paid to do it.

Theme 3: You Need To Train Your Mind For Success

Here we look at the power of your unconscious mind over your conscious one; how your life is controlled by your *seven CEOs* (who I will introduce later on in the book in detail); and why today is the perfect time to start updating your beliefs and social paradigms, to de-clutter your brain with a mindset shift and update your limiting beliefs. But, in order to do this, you must be willing to be uncomfortable for a while – the discomfort is just temporary, but the rewards are for the rest of your life.

So this means unlearning what you know and rewiring your mind to create new realities that will open your eyes to new opportunities. By developing your agility and flexibility to change and building your emotional resilience you will be giving yourself a tremendous competitive advantage and an invaluable skill for life.

Theme 4: You Need To Get The Right Support

It's tough going it alone so you will need emotional support to prevent your environment, your family, friends and society from pulling you back and stopping you moving forward. And, you will need to give yourself the time to build your emotional resilience so you know you can handle whatever comes your way. If you are to grow and expand and fly like an Eagle, you will need to invest in yourself by surrounding yourself with like-minded forward thinkers who believe in you.

Getting Ready To Learn And Adapt…

In order to know what you need to do differently you must first understand where you are right now in your life and how you have managed to get into your current situation, something we will look at over the next chapters.

Key Ideas to Take Away

1. If you are a typical professional, your upbringing and education up to now will not have prepared you for the brave new world of work that has arrived at your doorstep.

2. If you are to become a New Entrepreneur who achieves success on your own terms, you will need to de-clutter your mind and unlearn the unhealthy habits, beliefs and paradigms that are keeping you trapped.

3. Money likes clarity, discipline and speed. So, to bring abundance into your life you need to reset your wealth speedometer to match your different way of thinking and the 'new' evolved you that you are soon to become. You can't do this off old foundations or with a mind full of cobwebs.

4. There are different seasons in your life and you have had experience of some more than others, but you need to be open to experiencing them all. After all, this is what life is about, constant change, so being adaptable and developing your creative and lateral thinking will enable you to see things from different perspectives.

5. You are not alone. Thousands of professionals are facing what you are going through. The difference between the Chickens and the Eagles is that the latter will do whatever it takes to learn to fly and soar! The Chickens will remain in their lives of mediocrity, apathy and conformity watching others leaving them behind. Your life is a manifestation of the choices you make, so you must become more focused on the present and conscious about the life choices you make.

Your Notes

In The Next Chapter...

You will discover how you have been brainwashed since the day you were born. How the process of education, socialisation and parental indoctrination impacts upon every one of your thoughts until the day you rebel and take control of your life and your mind. You also need to become aware of the subtle ways in which the media, your peers and your working context shape your reality and your personality. That nothing is what it seems means that you need to start asking yourself powerful questions before giving your power and will away to others, because in doing this you give away your most precious gift: your soul.

Chapter 2

What A Mess

How To Understand YOUR Present

We are not born to live a boring and insignificant life that leaves less trace upon the planet than an ant. You are a unique and amazing work of art and well able to perform the most extraordinary tasks. However, somehow your everyday existence feels very different from the extraordinary. So what has happened to you?

Like many professionals, you feel trapped in a life that is not yours. We believe we are social beings, yet by living in a community, interacting with others and seeking them out we forget that we are individuals, and instead behave like parasites who depend on one another, taking more from others than we create together.

Of course, it's healthy to develop communities to live in; however, what we often create and experience is something quite different as we cram ourselves onto ever smaller pieces of land all fighting and competing for the same space.

But to me, living in a community means creating a space where a group of people who are self-sufficient and independent decide to bond together through choice, and not by a desire or need to live in proximity with others so *they* can provide for *you*.

Yet society makes an enormous and ongoing effort to ensure you conform, and so you do become smaller than an ant, leaving your individuality outside the door of the very first school you went to.

The same happens with most of your jobs.

As soon as you are hired it's as if you become the property of someone else with your surname changed to that of the company's.

In most large corporations, this starts with the company induction. From that moment on you are absorbing the company's culture, acquiring its values and having to align your objectives and goals to corporate policy. Company processes and procedures define the way you think and act, in some cases even down to the way you look and dress. If you weren't living in the West, they would have you sing the company song first thing in the morning.

No wonder that soon your identity starts to be assimilated by that of the company, and unless you fight to remain who you are from day one, you lose yourself in a trance that's induced by others.

But how is this all organised in the first place?

You Are Seduced By Shiny Objects And Glitter

You know how babies love colourful toys or anything that makes sound or noise. It's crucial in the development of their senses and helps them differentiate the information coming from the external world through so many different channels. So, in case you didn't know, boys like blue and girls like pink, and if you parents couldn't make up their minds you wore yellow. All sorted from day one.

As children we love presents, to be given gifts for any reason just because. Restaurants want to keep you happy giving you colouring books to keep you entertained so your parents keep coming back. Patisseries give young ones sweets so parents make them a frequent port of call. And so the whole system becomes one big market where anybody or anything that moves becomes a target.

By the time you are a teenager you are already well trained on how to manipulate adults to get what you want. But by this stage you want even more, you want the best and the most expensive things around, not just toys but gadgets. You want everything that your friends have, anything that is new, fancy, glossy, you just want more, 'more of whatever', it doesn't matter… peer pressure has started and it becomes stronger and stronger all the time.

As adults it's much the same, only the transactional value of the 'must haves' has increased. Now it's that new TV you don't need; then another car because the one you have is not the right shade of blue, or fast enough. So the story repeats.

This applies to us all, without exception, and the story will continue until you become the master of your own mind and start taking the decisions that matter most in your life.

But achieving such mastery doesn't happen by accident, it can only happen through choice, self-development and willpower. Just as the Eagle found, this is never easy but always necessary if you are not only to survive but to live and thrive!

You Believe The News!

Every day you take in the news so that you know what is going on and can talk about *important* things with others; it shows that you are current, responsible and cultivated. The problem with this is that you are being unconsciously manipulated daily, because what you are hearing or reading is not really *the* news at all but what others want you to focus on.

I notice that the more gloom and doom there is in politics, the economy or whatever, the more that football and other distractions are shown on TV. Sudden scandals or irrelevant facts about someone apparently important also become the main headlines so people lose track of what matters as their minds are directed more and more to what is actually irrelevant noise.

Every day you continue to do this, every time you accept what others say without question, the more you give away your power, the more it makes it easier for others to control you, your thoughts, your behaviour, your desires and wants.

It's as if somebody else – the media, the marketers, the news editors – is hijacking your identity – thinking and choosing for you... until you don't even know what your views really are any more, apart from what you are going to have for lunch. Even this can become too much of a choice, which is why you end up having pretty much the same, day in, day out. The purpose of all this is that you stop thinking for yourself.

Now, let me tell you a story that illustrates this perfectly.

The Socrates Filter Test

In Ancient Greece, the philosopher Socrates, who held knowledge in the highest esteem, was asked by a man he met one day: 'Do you know what I just heard about your friend?'

'Before you tell me,' said Socrates, 'I'd like you to take a little test. It's called the triple filter test.'

'Triple filter?' said the man.

'Yes,' said Socrates. 'I want you to pass what you are going to tell me through three filters, the first of which is truth. Are you willing to do this?'

'Yes,' said the man.

'Very well,' said Socrates, 'then let me ask you: have you made absolutely certain that what you are about to tell me is true?'

'No,' the man said, 'I've just heard about it and...,'

'So, as you do not really know if it's true or not, let us apply the second filter. Is what you are about to tell me about my friend something good?'

'No, quite the contrary,' said the man.

'So,' said Socrates, 'you want to tell me something bad about him, but you're not sure that it is true. You may still pass the test though, because there's one filter left: the filter of usefulness. Is what you want to tell me about my friend going to be useful to me?'

'No, not really,' said the man.

'Well,' concluded Socrates, 'if what you want to tell me is not true nor good nor even useful, why tell it to me at all?'

> **Exercise 3**
>
> It is time to take stock, so get your notepad ready, or use the notes section below to answer these questions, and write down what comes into your mind first.
>
> 1. What is the above story trying to tell you?
> 2. How does this story relate to you, to your habits and to what you do without even thinking twice?
> 3. Now what 'non-thinking' actions could you get rid of and do differently? Be specific. For instance, this could mean cutting down your TV viewing time to just an hour or two a week. Or watching only programmes that are worth watching. Or being choosy about what you read. Or deciding to stop gossiping about others.
> 4. Write down today's date by the side of your notes so you can compare your answers the next time you consider this story.

Your Notes

Do you realise how you are allowing your life to pass you by just sitting in front of a television that keeps drawing your attention to things that don't matter?

I can't stand TV, in fact I haven't had one for many years. I have never been a fan of allowing others to tell me what to do or what to buy, or even worse what to think. Unfortunately, my ex-husband apparently couldn't live without one in every room so I had to endure years of torturous television noise which left me feeling exhausted all the time. So, every day, I wanted to do less and at the weekends my only dream was to catch up on my sleep in order to keep going through the next week.

Of course, that weekend dream never happened because he was either watching TV in bed, or I would be woken by the sound of the radio news.

I didn't know how much all this was affecting me because my unconscious mind was preserving my sanity by trying to block out all this noise, something that required extra effort 24/7 on top of dealing with everything else in my life and all at the same time.

The problem was that when I fell asleep listening to the news in the background it affected my sleep patterns, as my mind was still processing all this information even though I wasn't aware of it. As a result, my energy levels were falling and my upbeat, outgoing and positive personality was fading. I was becoming unhappier, smiling less often, and becoming grumpier by the day. I was losing myself and becoming a reflection of those I was surrounded by.

The point I'm making here is that it's not just the impact of the media, TV and newspapers that you need to become aware of, but also of the impact that loved ones have on your life. But it's easier to see all their negativity for what it is when it is far away and more challenging when it is inside your own home.

As you move forward and make changes in your life you will find that the relationships with your close ones also change. This brings a challenge and an opportunity. If you support each other's dreams thorough your journey you will grow together stronger as a result. Otherwise you will be pulled apart.

I only realised how toxic my environment was after ten years when finally I divorced. I remember being in my little new flat listening to the silence. At the beginning, this was a bit overwhelming and the silence intensified this reality.

But I chose to struggle with being just me, grateful for the opportunity to find again those parts of me that had been left behind through those years. I knew that I needed to train my mind to distinguish between being alone and being lonely, and that if I wanted others to enjoy my company I needed to love myself first.

I knew I needed to make a choice and I chose to go through a process of rebirth like the Eagle so I could fly higher and further next time.

I had great friends, though most of them were in Spain, my parents had passed away and my closest family had their lives all organised. I have never been a dependent person even in the more tragic moments of my life. I have always known that I have an enormous resilience and an inner strength that nobody can destroy, my spirit keeps lifting me up time after time. Just realising this made me aware that I wasn't so lost after all. I knew who I was (I only needed to collect the bits left behind), and this is the most powerful weapon any human being can ever possess.

Forget the nuclear bomb, this is for people, even worse for nations who don't know who they are and what they stand for and live always with fear, scared of what others may or may not do. They always need something external to protect them even though real strength comes from inside.

You Follow The Celebrities And The Glossy Magazines

Yes, the glossy magazines, the weekly or monthly dose of gossip about somebody else's life. While you're bothering so much about other lives you don't need to look at what is happening in yours. You dream about other lives because you can't be bothered to create your own. You see yourself either as so different from them that you believe these things will never happen to you, or you become so infatuated and self-centred about how amazing you are (even though you have probably achieved little) that you believe you can have it all, just because.

Neither this inability to create your own life, or your self-infatuation, is totally your fault, after all you are just the sum of the social inputs you have been receiving since being a child, and which are reinforced every day, day in, day out, in so many different ways. Listening to others for instructions and orders on what to do; and always desiring what others have without thinking if you really want or need it; or feeling that what matters is to be the same as others, is the result.

This can make you feel that you are the same as an 'achiever' even though you are not prepared to put in their efforts to get certain results. Sorry, but this is nothing more than pure fantasy.

Our thinking systems are this shallow because when you asked people questions they didn't like or to which they had no answer, you were quickly put in your place and told to shut up, explicitly and implicitly with social putdowns.

As you know, the mind learns through repetition, so every time this happened, 'shutting up' became a pattern that today impacts on every area of your life, a pattern that will remain until you learn how to change it.

And as shutting up became the norm, your voice grew quieter, until it can now barely be heard. You have become invisible, lost in the shadows of all the celebrities and bling that is around you.

The media, television, corporate employers, the influence of some of your closest relationships, all-pervasive celebrities and a 'must have now' culture all contribute to filling your mind full of noise and manipulating the way you think so you conform. This makes it difficult to fully understand what you want in your life and who you really are.

For example, let's look now at one of the biggest decisions you have ever made in your life, and how you came to have the least influence on what was decided.

You Wanted The Easy Gold

As we grow up, the social pressure on us to decide what we want to do for the rest of our lives becomes enormous. But you need to find an answer to this question as fast as possible before your parents and teachers lose their patience with you for not knowing.

This is one of the most important decisions you will make in your life, yet you are given just a few months to come up with a congruent and absolute answer!

Looking back on this, you can clearly see that it is a nonsensical scenario and a perfect platform for disaster, especially when you are not given useful guidance at all.

Being told: 'Why don't you study IT, you are great with computers?' or, 'Why don't you become a lawyer like your father?' or, 'Why don't you carry on the family business?' is not useful advice but manipulation so you will conform to social norms and expectations. It's much easier for others to tell you what to do rather than helping you take the time to fully understand who you are and what you are passionate about. Doing the same as previous generations seems easier still –after all you will be walking a well-trodden road.

So, you take a decision that is going to shape at least half of your life – unless you die an early metaphorical death through despair, frustration or boredom and become emotionally and spiritually one of the 'walking dead' whose dreams are so far distant that they can't even be remembered.

If your family and friends don't manage to persuade you along a chosen route then psychometric tests, the press and futurists will probably do it for you.

'They' don't give you guidelines on how to make a living, or create a life doing something you are passionate about and love. Instead, *'they'* tell you about the jobs and professions *'they'* think are best choices for you if you want to succeed. And to 'help', they give you a list of subjects and you're told to pick one based on a future that nobody knows.

So you pick from the list that has been created by somebody you have probably never met and who certainly knows little about you. But you trust them because they know best, after all, they are the 'experts'. There's only one problem. How can anybody be an expert on you, except YOU? Unless, of course, you don't even know who you are.

It's You Who Allows Others To Choose For You

How Did You Lose Your Voice?

As mentioned before, we are born as social beings who need to interact with others, which is great as far as these others allow you to be yourself at the same time as being part of the community.

Unfortunately, being accepted as part of a group comes with a lot of rules, the main one of which is: 'You must be like us if you want to stay'. Of course, what you don't appreciate is that this is a two-way street. It's not just a case of if they want you, but also whether you want them.

After all, you can always create your own community, or allow yourself the freedom to be found by another community to which you can better relate. So, there is never a need to trade your identity for anybody else's approval, no matter how important they are – or think they are – after all they are just mortal people too.

So, let's get a bit more clarity about how you managed to get to where you are today, because nothing is by accident, it's always by design.

Which Values Did You Trade For Love?

You want to be accepted because it makes you feel good and makes your life a whole lot easier. However, when you become someone other than your real self, to have a sense of belonging, something doesn't feel quite right.

But this is what you've done the whole time with your parents, your siblings, your friends, your teachers, your colleagues and your boss because you want to be acknowledged, to be seen and to be recognised by them, and you paid a high price for this. Didn't you?

When I was 17 I was madly in love with a boy my age. He was very handsome and smart, and at the time I would do anything I could (within my own sense of respect and self worth) to bring myself to his attention. So, I would go to the places he liked to go, socialise with his friends, even though their interests and values didn't align with mine; and drink a little, even though I have never enjoyed it much.

I became a 'pleaser' for someone who didn't matter and who didn't love me; in fact, he only loved himself.

I realised then that love has nothing to do with moving away from yourself, but rather the opposite, love brings you closer to who you truly are.

Thanks to this painful experience, and others that came later, I am today in the most amazing relationship any human being could experience in a lifetime.

For this I am grateful.

Exercise 4

Get ready to write the answers in your notepad or Resources Pack. If you haven't downloaded one yet, go to: **www.maitebaron.com/resource-pack**

1. What values have you traded for love?

2. How did you become a pleaser?

3. How did you forget about your own needs?

Or, maybe it wasn't love that stopped you being yourself but money, so:

4. What dreams did you give up for money?

5. Did you study a career just for the money?

6. Did you make a choice based on someone else's dream?

7. Did you choose to go into the family business because it just felt easier?

Your Notes

My mother wanted to be a doctor but was not allowed to because my grandfather had already decided that her purpose in life would be to get married and have children. However, being creative and loving clothes, my mother hoped she would be able to study fashion, but unfortunately for my grandfather even this was too artistic, bohemian and definitely not a choice for a decent woman. My mother insisted that she wanted to do something and so finally was allowed to study commerce. This didn't interest her one bit, but at least it was thought that this might be useful for the family business... while she was still single. My mother married at the age of 27, considered pretty late for her generation, and the next day stopped working and became a housewife for life. This was her wedding present!

With her passion and creativity given away, my mother tried to fill in the gap with artistic courses and cooking, at which she did brilliantly, creating a home that was full of beauty and balance and above all tons of love.

But even though she had a good life by many standards, she never fulfilled her life's purpose. Some may think she gave up her life in the name of love, but I find it difficult to believe this nonsense. She was manipulated by my grandfather and then by my father, who held the same traditional beliefs, to suit their needs, enabling them to succeed professionally because everything else was taken care of by her.

Exercise 5

Answer these questions in your Resources Pack (you can download this at **www.maitebaron.com/resourcepack**), just noting what comes to you.

1. Does the above story resonate with you?

2. In your personal life, which is the role you have played so far in your relationships with your partner, your parents, your siblings, your friends? The dominator or the dominated?

3. At work, which is the role you have played so far, with your boss, your clients and your colleagues? The dominator or the dominated?

Your Notes

Let's get back to the heart of things.

What Did You Leave Behind To Be Accepted Or To Be Like Everyone Else?

Answer the following questions, and circle the answer that best suits.

Do you feel free?	Yes / No
Do you feel good about the different aspects of your life?	Yes / No
Do you wake up every morning feeling excited about the new day?	Yes / No
Do you feel alive?	Yes / No
Do you go through life feeling the 'wow!' factor, looking for new experiences and exhilarated about the difference you can make every day to yourself and others?	Yes / No

I suspect most of your answers were 'No's', right? So, let's find out what's keeping you stuck or unhappy in different areas of your life.

> ### Exercise 6
> Once you are ready, answer these three questions allowing the responses to come to you naturally and in their own time. Don't judge the answers; just write them down allowing yourself to go deeper and deeper into your thought process.
>
> 1. How are you currently trading freedom for conformity in your life right now?
> 2. How are you currently trading excitement for mediocrity in your life right now?
> 3. How are you currently trading feeling alive for apathy in your life right now?

What did you notice as you answered the questions?

How do you feel about your answers?

If you don't like the answers, what are you going to do about it? Be specific by coming up with a numbered list of action points. Write down today's date beside them so that you can keep an eye on how you are progressing towards them.

Your Notes

....

....

....

....

....

....

You Took A Road Already Travelled

Perhaps you initially believed your career choice was just a temporary decision, one to which you weren't fully committed, but nevertheless a foot on the career ladder.

But you worked hard because you had an overall plan: find somebody to be with, get married, buy a house, work harder to get promoted, then after that 'I will do what I love with my life'.

Twenty years along the line you are tired, you have stopped believing that your life will get any better and you have put your dreams on hold forever.

In reality, you started giving up your dreams the first time you were seduced by someone else's story. You forgot who you were and started to follow the crowd, taking someone else's road, just so you could become more like others.

So, you have worked hard to be where you are but still there is a feeling that something is missing, that you are sleepwalking through a life that is distant and detached from everything around you.

You Feel Trapped And You're Not The Only One

Now, after all this effort, you have a job, a mortgage, a partner and all the rest, so from the outside there is nothing wrong with you and how your life has worked out so far. In fact, some of your colleagues may even see you as an example of what they want to achieve because to them you represent success.

The real crack is inside. 'Is this it? Is there no more to life than to keep repeating your daily routine until the day you die? Are you just passing through life, not really alive at all?'

The Truth Is You Have Had Enough

You keep telling yourself that when the kids grow up you will do something 'you want for a change'. And that when you get the next promotion you will pay off your mortgage so you can feel free. And that when your partner goes back to working more hours you will feel under less pressure and be better able to relax. And that when your parents feel better (or are dead) you can relocate to somewhere you want to be. But all of this is nothing more than delusional self talk that will keep you trapped forever.

Every 'yes' and 'but' and 'when' and 'then' is nothing more than an aspirin to anaesthetise the pain of truth – your life is permanently on hold. If you're thinking all this sounds melodramatic, a bit over the top, things can't really be that bad, then you may be more deluded than you think.

At a deep level you are already aware of this… but you don't know what to do about it.

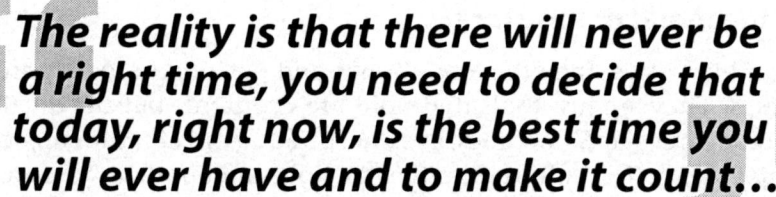

> *The reality is that there will never be a right time, you need to decide that today, right now, is the best time you will ever have and to make it count...*

You Feel Confused And It's Normal

You feel stuck in a double bind. Your mind tells you to stick with what you know; after all, why throw away everything you have been working so hard for? On the other hand, your heart is aching with restlessness and unfulfillment. Your soul is crying out for something different. What it wants is for you to have your life back, to have the courage to make your dreams come true. It wants you to find yourself again.

Let me share this story with you, which will help to throw more light on the situation you are facing.

The Professor And The Alumni

Now all well established in their careers, a group of alumni return to visit an old university professor. Conversation soon turns into complaints about the stress of work and life.

Offering his guests coffee, the professor goes to the kitchen and returns with a large pot and an assortment of cups – porcelain, plastic, glass, crystal, some plain, others expensive and exquisite – and he tells his guests to help themselves to hot coffee.

When all the students have a cup in their hands, the professor looks around at them all and says: 'If you notice, all of you have taken a nice looking or expensive cup and have left behind the plain and cheap ones. While it is normal for you to seek only the best for yourselves, all that you actually wanted was the coffee, not the cup. But you unconsciously went for the best cups and then spent your time eyeing up each other's. This shows you the source of your stress.'

And the moral of this story?

If life is like coffee, then the jobs, money and position in society are like the cups. They are just tools that hold life's contents but the quality of life doesn't change. Sometimes, by concentrating only on the cup, we fail to enjoy the coffee in it, so don't let the love of cups drive you... enjoy the coffee instead.

> **Exercise 7**
>
> 1. What insights came to you from this story?

Your Notes

....

....

....

....

....

You Feel Disorientated And It Makes Sense

Every day you stop and reflect on your life, you know you are living a big lie, that you are living someone else's existence but not yours. The main character in the film of your life looks like you, dresses like you, but feels lost, confused, disorientated and scared.

You feel your life running through your fingers like sand. You know you are not using your full potential and that you are just ticking along. And so you close your mind to the problem by being busy, running around like a headless chicken and feeling important because your to-do list is so long. After all, if you have such a busy life, this must mean that you are at least successful at one level, that you must exist.

So, you can't let go of all the things in your life, even the ones that don't mean much to you. But all these things just steal your life away like a 'time vampire' and you are getting no pleasure in return.

Others around you will tell you it's too late, that you *are* like everyone else, and that you shouldn't complain!

And then you feel guilty because in comparison with others your life seems OK, and anyway you chose this path didn't you, so the easiest thing to do is to stick at it and keep going, ignoring what your heart and soul tell you every day… that you are being untruthful to yourself. It feels all quite shallow and pointless, but you are too scared to start again.

You have people around you but you feel disconnected from them. At work you are in the same space as colleagues to whom you don't relate, while at home the relationship with your partner has just become routine. You now have little in common as you have grown apart and have developed an ordinary relationship in which nothing important is ever exchanged. In fact, you try to avoid the important topics in case a spark from one ignites a fire and everything goes up in flames.

I remember waking up each morning feeling as though my body weighed three tons or more, needing a crane to lift it up from the bed. I would brush my teeth, have a shower, eat a quick breakfast and walk fast through the streets to make sure I could catch the first tube train that came along. I remember seeing things and people around me as though they were moving in slow motion, as if the colours of the world had disappeared to leave behind just a palette of black and white with greys in between.

And then as I was walking through the underground station, I would see a huge advertisement poster saying: 'There is light at the end of the tunnel', and it felt like this was directed at me, as if a strange force wanted to give me some hope.

I repeated these 'words' to myself on my way to the college where I taught at the time and it kept me going for a while, but eventually I had to confront the truth. I was not happy in my relationship, and while the teaching part of my job was good, as I was helping people progress through life and giving people hope about their future, there was always the bureaucracy that forced me to follow someone else's path. And why was I doing this? Just to contribute to my partner's mortgage!

My relationship with him had also become hostile. In essence, I had disharmony in my heart, I was living my life by dishonouring my more cherished values. I was living a lie in every sense and I felt terribly upset and lost.

But 'there is light at the end of the tunnel' I kept telling myself while I was carrying on living a life that was not mine.

When Did You Stop Being A Leader And Became A Follower?

> *You will notice that I often use the word Leader in this book, by which I mean Self-Leadership as I can't understand how any human being not in charge of their own life can pretend to lead others. Leadership is an art and its mastery starts with the Self*

I write the Leader word with a capital 'L', not by accident. In today's world where everybody wants to influence how you think, live and feel, being yourself is one the biggest challenges you can face. So, being able to live by your values, knowing who you are and what you want is one of the greatest successes you can ever achieve.

My aim is to waken the Eagle in you, to help you rise and fly as this is what being a Leader is about, leading your own life and by doing so inspiring others to have the courage to do the same.

So, why continue to care so much about what others think, say or believe about you? Why should people you don't even know matter at all to you? Is it just because we are social beings with a need to belong that is so strong we are willing to sell ourselves, our life, our heart and our soul to be one with others, or is there something deeper going on?

You Have Started Believing That 'You're Not Good Enough'

You have since childhood been manipulated and controlled by your parents, the rest of your family, your teachers, your friends, your environment, by society, by conformity and mediocrity, by bureaucracy and by authority. Indeed, anybody and anything that could claim a part of you has done so.

Of course, they mostly did this with the best of intentions, but nevertheless they interfered with the development of your identity and what you stand for as an individual in the world.

Slowly, you gave up the responsibility to choose for yourself, as it became the norm to meet everyone else's needs and wants first. As a result, you have started believing that you are not good enough and that others know better and so should decide for you. You believed you couldn't have what you wanted so you compromised.

This pattern keeps repeating in different areas of your life, doesn't it? But you already know that you can't go on like this forever. Don't you?

At one point you did want to do something with your life, to be someone, you were excited about finding something special that was just waiting to make your life great. Then the opinions, ideas and failed dreams of others came your way. They told you that your ideas were crazy, that what you wanted to do was impossible for you to achieve; that you were OK in a certain field but not good enough to make it to the top, or to earn a living from your dream. What was the point in struggling all your life when you could follow an easy path? They kept on telling you this and you kept on listening.

So you parked up your dreams and you conformed. You did once more what you were told and this is the story that has been repeating itself ever since. Deep down you could say to yourself that if this didn't work out, then at least you would have someone to blame, which is always easier than taking responsibility for yourself. Unfortunately, this is what most people choose to do.

You Were Scared To Be Yourself

As a social being you've always wanted to conform since you don't want to be alone but to have friends and people to go out with at the weekends, to have a boyfriend or girlfriend just like everybody else. You want to be popular and in demand.

So you did what you could to be noticed by your peer group, you tried to blend in, to be one like them, and because you were scared that they might find out that you were different from them, you made sure that you didn't stand out.

The good news is that when you discover who you truly are and accept this with all of your heart, then you are on the path to experiencing real freedom, which is when your life really begins!

Your road to conformity started as a child at school with your teachers making sure they didn't do anything to impact your marks; then as a teenager; then with your first intimate relationship; then with your friends; then with your parents; and now you are at 40+ still playing this game at work.

But now you are given a second chance:

What would you do with an amazing opportunity to turn your life around? To be an Eagle ready to fly to different lands and heights rather than a Chicken with its head down pecking grain in the sand?

I remember battling with my parents, especially my father, because their views were very traditional and old-fashioned. I didn't want to be controlled, as my mother had been, by other people's social values, but they still tried to educate me to become the perfect housewife, something that as far as I can remember had never been my dream, far from it.

As a child I wanted to play with the Scalextric and trains, but instead at Christmas the Three Kings from the Orient (I'm Spanish Catholic) brought me dolls and a sewing machine and this drove me nuts. When I was six, I remember telling my parents that if the Three Kings were so wise, how come they managed to always bring me the wrong toys, especially as I was a good girl who wrote them a letter telling them specifically what I wanted?

My father used to get upset when I stood up to him for what I wanted and believed in, because he felt this threatened his authority, which was not my intention at all. What adults never seem to get is that as a child you can already see what is nonsense, so asking me to do certain things, 'just because', made no sense at all so why obey?

At school, I was labeled as 'creative', which meant they didn't know what to do with me, and this at a Catholic school that preached about accepting people as they are and goodwill to all.

I realise now how lucky I was to go to this school, even though the nuns greatly annoyed me with their rituals and forced attendance at church. However, they did what they preached and they gave me roots, a belief system that I could choose if I wished, and above all plenty of love and care, in their own way. They didn't force me to become someone else.

I created friendships then which are alive today, true friendships that have overcome all the odds. But I always felt different, my dream was not to fit in with the social norms but to create my own way, to make a difference in the world, to live an exciting life where things are better because I was there.

I did go to university and I studied psychology for two years but left feeling disappointed and disenchanted with the whole experience as all my psychology teachers seemed 'numb' and even less happy than I was. Just the remote possibility of becoming like them after five years of indoctrination scared me to the point of making me want to leave and find my own way before it was too late.

> **Key Ideas To Take Away**
>
> 1. Society will do what it can to manipulate and control your mind. It's much easier to deal with followers than it is to create Leaders (professionals who lead themselves and are able to make their own choices and take their own decisions). We are heading towards a society where Self-Leaders are the only ones in control of their lives. You have to decide if you want to be one of these New Entrepreneurs who choose to live with purpose and prosperity or to be just one more in the crowd.
>
> 2. You need to take responsibility for your own life and not allow others to choose it for you. This applies to every area of your life, without exception.
>
> 3. Nothing happens by accident. Every day you make decisions that shape the life you live, so make sure that these are conscious and based on your values and what you want to experience more in your life.
>
> 4. TV, gossip and the news clutter the mind and take power away from you. Make sure that doesn't happen by feeding it with quality rather than quantity. Be choosy because it matters!
>
> 5. When you know who you are, you will never feel alone. So, invest in your own self-development because this is the best return on investment by a thousand times that you can make. Choose to be an Eagle and learn to fly otherwise you will end up on the barbecue with all the other Chickens!

In The Next Chapter...

You will discover how your daily experience is nothing less than a direct response to who you are, how you respond to your environment, the people around you, and the beliefs you hold. You will also learn how the pursuit of security, comfort and stability is a great recipe for conformity, apathy and mediocrity, leading to an undeveloped and unexplored life, where aspirations, creativity and, worst of all, dreams, are killed.

Chapter 3

Reality Doesn't Exist... Really

You See The World Not As It Is, But As You Are

You occupy the same physical space as others, but you notice and experience different things even at the same time.

This means that your life experience is shaping your viewpoint as if you were wearing glasses with your own set of lenses, perceiving a partial reality.

Every day you have the opportunity to clear your lenses through new experiences in a fresh way, updating the distorted memories that are hidden away and locked in your mind.

Your Beliefs About Others Become The Essence Of Your Relationships

Since childhood all your memories rest in your mind waiting for triggers to unlock them.

So, if you have learned to believe that people like you, then you will find it easy to make friends and to talk to strangers. On the other hand, if you believe that people *don't* like you, then you will feel inadequate.

But, what would happen if you believed yourself so lovable that everyone could find you irresistible? How would your life be then?

The point is that you are free to choose how you feel about people at any given time. This choice is important because it shapes both your personal and professional relationships and, as a result, the overall quality of your life.

As a Leader, your beliefs about people come across through each and every interaction you make with them. This means it's not enough just to want to be liked by others and like people too, you have to make that choice from your heart. If you care, so will they. This is something that you can't fake because your beliefs don't need words to be heard by others.

Let me now introduce you to the concept of mirror neurons, considered to be one of the most important neuroscience discoveries of the last decade.

The human brain has multiple mirror neuron systems that specialise in understanding others' intentions, not just their actions, but also the social meaning of their behaviour and their emotions.

So, when you watch someone performing an action – say moving a chair – the mirror neurons in your brain simulate that action and create a template for anticipating what will happen next. Because of these mirror neurons, you can read people's intentions. This allows you to empathise with them because you are able to feel quite literally what they are feeling.

Have you ever entered a room where an argument has taken place and as soon as you walked in you could feel that something had happened?

Your Perceptions Of The World Create Both An Ocean Of Possibilities Or A Desert Of Deadness. You Choose.

When you are out and about in the world, living in a big city, interacting with strangers walking by, you can see different colours, ages and shapes.

If, when seeing a multicultural crowd, you start being discriminating about people, even unconsciously, in your world you will create disharmony. If you feel uneasy in the presence of different cultures and ideologies and only notice what is different, you will create distance and separation between people. And ultimately taken to extremes, this sort of thinking can lead to war.

Sometimes you hear people saying: 'All white people are like this', or 'All black people are like that', as if the world was this simple. Instead, we are all unique, with much to contribute to one another, if we are given the chance to express ourselves without the need to apologise for having a 'package' that is right or wrong depending on your perception.

On the other hand, if when seeing people that are different from you, you are also able to see the similarities, the beauty is that the differences will then quickly disappear.

Time for an insight from a Chinese Fable

A water bearer in China had two large pots. Each hung from the end of a yoke he carried about his neck. While one of the pots was perfect in every detail, the other was cracked.

This meant that the bearer, after a long walk back from the stream to his house, could only ever return with one and a half pots of water.

Of course, the perfect pot didn't mind this at all and was proud of its accomplishments. However, the cracked pot was ashamed of its imperfection, miserable that it was able to accomplish only half of what it was made to do. So, after two years of what it perceived to be its bitter failure, the cracked pot finally spoke to the water bearer as he stood by the stream.

'I am ashamed of myself,' said the pot, 'because this crack in my side means water leaks out all the way back to your house.'

The bearer replied: 'Did you never notice that there were flowers only on your side of the path, but not on the other? I have always known about your flaw, which is why I planted flower seeds only on your side of the path so that every day while we walked back from the stream you would be watering them. So, for two years I have been able to pick these beautiful flowers to decorate my table. Without you being the way you are, all of their beauty that graces my house would not have been possible.'

And the moral of this story?

We're all cracked pots in our own way with our own unique flaws. But it's these imperfections that make our lives together so interesting.

> **Exercise 8**
> 1. What are the flaws you keep complaining about?
> 2. How could you use these flaws to advantage? In what circumstances would they be a strength that you could draw on?
> 3. Now, how do you see these flaws? As a problem or as a potential opportunity?

Your Notes

....

....

....

....

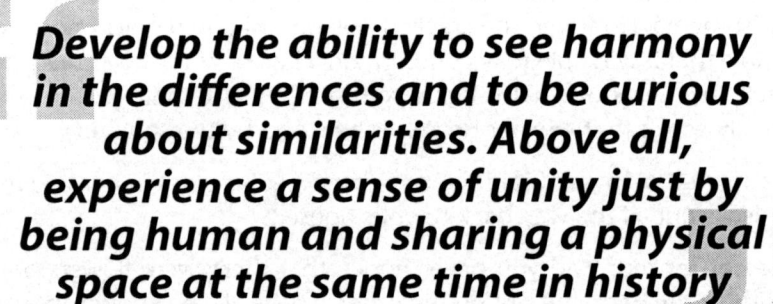

Develop the ability to see harmony in the differences and to be curious about similarities. Above all, experience a sense of unity just by being human and sharing a physical space at the same time in history

What You Think About In Life Becomes Your Daily Reality

You encounter people all day long; for some, things just seem to happen, it looks like they were born on the right day, under the right stars. People love them; they seem to get on with anybody and everybody. It feels good to be around them; they have a positive energy that is contagious. There is always something good going on in their life. You call them lucky.

Then there are others who are endlessly nagging, they are draining and dragging, everything is wrong in and with their world which is always full of rain and clouds. As a result, you try to spend as little time as possible with them, unless of course their thoughts resonate with yours because you think the same!

Yet none of these individuals was born lucky or unlucky. The only difference between them is that those who are positive make the most of what they have, while those who are negative only see the bad in life. The great thing is that you can be either of these two types, the choice is yours.

If you believe that life is hard and that you need to hold onto whatever comes along because you have no other choice, then yes, your life is going to be hard. On the other hand, if you believe that life is a long exciting journey, then yes, your life will be like this because you won't judge things as being good or bad but as events that happen through life to help you explore different aspects of yourself and the world around you.

If you believe that life brings you perfect opportunities to grow, then you will be open to approach each day's events with the curiosity of the child who allows things to unfold before them without needing everything to be planned before they feel safe and secure.

Here's a simple story that will help shift your perspective so you see this bigger picture.

The Hindu Master

An ageing Hindu master was growing tired of his apprentice complaining, so one morning he instructed the unhappy young man to put a handful of salt in a glass of water and then drink it.

'How does it taste?' the Hindu Master asked.

'Bitter,' said the apprentice spitting out the salty water.

The master then asked the young man to take another handful of salt and this time to put it into a nearby lake, which the apprentice did.

'Now drink from the lake,' said the Hindu Master.

As the water dripped down the young man's chin, the Hindu Master asked: 'How does that taste?'

'Fresh,' replied the apprentice.

'Did you taste the salt?' said the Hindu Master.

'No,' said the young man.

'Then now you realise that the pain of life is pure salt; no more, no less,' explained the Hindu Master.

And the moral of this story?

The amount of pain in life remains always the same. However, the amount of bitterness we taste depends on the container we put the pain in. So when you are in pain, the only thing you can do is to enlarge your sense of things. Stop being a glass and become a lake.

> **Exercise 9**
> 1. What is the glass of salt water in your own life?
> 2. And how can you transform this glass into the lake?

Your Notes

....

....

....

....

....

At any time that you can shift your perspective and see your current pain in the context of the bigger picture of your life you are able to free yourself up from that pain. As you can imagine, this is a skill worth developing, so let's start practicing.

The Pursuit Of Security Is A Fallacy

Security doesn't physically exist, you just create the feeling in your mind which then becomes real because you believe it. As a mechanism this may help you cope with daily events, but as a feeling it is just a fallacy, a fantasy created by our social beliefs in order to keep repeating what you do without questioning it – a great recipe for mediocrity.

How Society Reinforces This Belief And Why?

The pursuit of work and domestic security can easily create a robotic-like existence that not only helps society (and the system) control you, but also enables you to avoid the responsibility of using your brain to think for yourself.

Everything around you is designed to reinforce this belief by creating a false sense of security. The media tells you what to think and they only need to convince you to buy X or Y newspaper for you to read what they want you to read, and this reinforces beliefs that are in most cases theirs not yours, but no matter, you feel good by being up-to-date, informed and so a good and responsible citizen.

The TV also tells you how to behave, when to stay passive and when to become active, such as at election times. The news then is coloured by the lens of the TV channel and the journalist who reports on these supposed events, some real and some manufactured.

Then the commercials tell you what to buy and pretend to make your shopping experience easier, even though you already know that this is far from being the case, particularly when they keep moving the stuff on the supermarket shelves, or a manufacturer has the same products, just branded with different packaging.

If this was not enough ongoing control and manipulation, let's add in the peer pressure that comes from friends and colleagues telling you exactly how to behave, what to do, where to go and how to dress if you want to 'belong' to their group or community.

If you are invited to go to the pub on a Friday night with your work colleagues, it looks as though you have a choice, but you don't. Keep missing these social gatherings and soon you will find that all the opportunities and promotions go to someone else, because it's clear that you are not the same as them, you are not fitting in, you are not controllable or predictable. The pub on Friday night has become a mobile office in disguise, where big brother is watching.

And don't forget about the football matches and golf games that others want you to play. Until you realise that your free time belongs to many others through such social 'obligations' and expectations, you won't find space for you in your life. The only thing you will notice is how your life is being eaten away and how your free time is planned in other's agendas and you are expected to conform.

The main objective here is that you don't have any quiet time when you can reflect on your life and the absurdity of the many practices you feel compelled to comply with. Thinking for yourself has in effect become a luxury.

You need to understand that all this conformity is what kills the entrepreneurial spirit. By being sucked into a world of conformity, mediocrity and apathy you stop being free to follow your dreams and become a New Entrepreneur. You need to claim your power back.

Why does society put so much effort into doing all this?

For starters, because you can only be controlled if you become a conformist who can only aspire to mediocrity by accepting what you are told as a matter of fact. Then routine, disengagement and apathy becomes your normal reaction to life's events. The objective of society is to control the masses, to strip you of your ability to think, to make sure that you don't have an opinion, or at least, don't dare to express it – and we call this democracy.

You may be thinking, what is she talking about? She has gone too far. What about all these polls and surveys that ask for my opinion? Yes, there are plenty of those around, often wanting to know irrelevant things that don't make your life or that of others any better, and all costing millions.

Do you really need a survey to measure people's levels of happiness to know what is going on? Can't you see the expression on their faces every day? Do they look happy to you? Have we forgotten what happiness looks like and so need to collect numbers to discover this?

What about climate change? Many 'influential' people are still debating if this is a problem at all, which makes your opinion on what to do about it irrelevant.

And labour laws? Too complicated. You are just a citizen who doesn't understand how these things work so it's better that someone else decides on your behalf. And this keeps going on and on…

It's crucial you become aware of your own paradigms, which are buried deeper than your simple habits and routines. These models of living are the cumulative effect of your family tree, your upbringing, your environment... even the 'social thinking' that is programmed into you by the media. These are your 'default programs', the ones that define both your potential and your limitations.

However, there is good news – it is perfectly possible to re-programme yourself and reset your mind, something we will look at how to do later, so stay with me for a bit. It is all fundamental to acquiring the thinking and the mindset that you need to succeed as New Entrepreneur. Get your thinking right and the rest will start to fall into place.

Remember, security doesn't exist! It's a fallacy to keep you hooked, and now that you know this, you can decide what you want to experience instead and use your energy to create the life that's best for you, instead of looking for safety. And you can do this starting today.

Let's start putting some of these thoughts into practice.

Action Steps

1. Start eliminating any negative influences from your thinking by deleting negative self-talk that tells you: 'I'm not good enough' or 'Nobody will listen to me', and replace these with positive phrases, such as: 'I will do my best at every opportunity' or 'I have something worth saying'. You have the power to choose.

2. Read books and articles that inspire you. Be choosy.

3. Surround yourself with people who encourage and believe in you, rather than those who constantly criticise. You will feel a surge in your energy!

4. Avoid reading newspapers and watching pulp TV programmes. Better still, stop watching TV and listening to the radio completely. If there is something so important, others will tell you. News travels fast.

5. Stop being brainwashed, and actively seek out new challenges and ideas. Never settle for anything less than living by your values! After all you are an Eagle, so stop behaving like a Chicken.

Your Notes

....

....

....

....

....

The Search For Comfort Kills Aspirations And Creativity

Another big lie is that an adult aspiration should be the search for comfort because this is what we are created for, and when we achieve it, we will have arrived! But arrived where? At Boredom City? On the planet of the walking dead?

You complain that your life is boring, that it feels like a black and white film. It's as if all the colours you saw as a child from a place of wonder and curiosity have been stripped away from your adult life since the day you left university and started working in the adult's world.

You don't have a zest for life anymore, everything feels a big effort, your life is so full of 'to do's', that you can't possibly take on one more thing.

Even when friends suggest a weekend away, you can't because you have something to finish for Monday, or because you are so exhausted that you can't move, or because you need to collect the shirts from the dry cleaner.

When will there ever be time for you? The answer looks like... never. And this is part of the problem.

Slowly, slowly, your life is so out of balance that this becomes the norm. Your whole body tries to keep up with your weekend drinking, detoxifying during the week, working out at the gym, dealing with lack of sleep, working hard, all the time you are running on a hamster wheel. And, because nearly everyone else seems to be doing the same, you assume that nothing's wrong.?

But in fact, your life has just become a 'repeat' of your past, rather than a continuous journey. Sometimes you feel like you actually are running around in circles, living 'a déjà vu existence', and you are right! You are in a permanent trance which you are not even aware of and in which you believe you are freely choosing every single action. But the truth is that, unless you live in the present and make conscious choices, that will never be the case.

Can you remember the last time you did something as ordinary as just drinking a glass of water and tasting every sip in your mouth, living that experience and nothing else? You may not even know what this feels like if you haven't experienced it, or have always lived your life in the regretted past, or in an imagined future.

If this is your reality then you're not choosing freely because others are choosing for you. To change this you need to wake up from your sleep-walking and start *being* in the present (I will show you how to do this later on in the book) as this is the only way to feel alive!

The Search For Stability Leads To An Unexplored Life

A close companion of security and conformity is stability, which strives to keep things as they are, so you experience few life changes by avoiding anything on the horizon that may hide a surprise.

And while temporary stability is a breathing space, where the life explorer in you can recharge batteries, stability isn't meant to be a permanent parking place. It's good, for a while but as soon as you feel like you are starting to stagnate this is a sign that you are ready to move on to whatever is next, whether that's learning a new language, taking a cookery class, visiting another country or volunteering for a cause – get engaged in something!

It will not only be good for your mind but will also spark your spirit. Being committed to your life is the best youth 'pill' you could ever take, and much cheaper than Botox or any of that rubbish.

I remember travelling in China in 1982. Then, it was not the modern country that is growing rapidly and evolving today. It was stuck in the past and life was tough for the majority of people. At the time they still had two currencies, one for the tourist and one for the residents. We were travelling around the country for a month and had a guide called Chao throughout the trip. He was paid a pittance, but then why would he need any more? His life was well controlled and all the basics were provided for him, so he had little to worry about.

One day, we were on a long train journey from Beijing to Xian to see the Terracotta Warriors. The train was hot, there was no air conditioning and only hot water was available to drink. The journey was long and we had plenty of time to talk. I asked Chao, what would he like to do if he could choose to do anything without worrying about money?

'I don't know,' he said.

'OK. What would you do or where would you go if you could leave China?' I asked.

'I don't know,' he replied.

'Have you ever dreamed about doing this?' I said.

'No, I don't even have a passport. What is the point of dreaming about things that can't happen?'

Chao was being a good citizen, brainwashed and completely unable to think or dream beyond his reality.

I felt sad and I thought: make sure this doesn't happen to you! You may be thinking, well if he is happy like this, what is the problem? You are right, if he was happy it wouldn't be a problem, but he wasn't. There wasn't much left of his human spirit, he was just going through the motions, unemotional, nearly robotic.

I wonder, how he is coping today in his fast-changing country?

Unfortunately, in our own democratic and free nations there are many Chaos, and I keep asking myself, how come?

Even in disorder there is stability when you know who you are and what you stand for. You may feel temporarily unsure about where the next destination is on your trip, but you know that there are options that will feel right for you. You may not know any details, or how to get there or who is going to be with you on the same path, but there is an inner knowledge that you will find the way. There may be elements of confusion and uneasiness but there is no panic. You trust your gut instinct and your intuition (if you haven't forgotten how to access it), and so can set your inner navigator to help you trace the new way forward for you.

Why What You Believe Really Matters

We have looked at how the system is designed from the moment you are born, to take control of your thoughts, feelings and individuality. So, by now you know that in order to live *your* life and become a New Entrepreneur you need to learn how to control your mind. More importantly, you need to get your unconscious mind to be your ally and guide, because your unconscious mind shapes your perceptions and your beliefs as it absorbs everything you turn your attention to.

The aim is for you to learn how to live from a place of being (not just doing), so that you become aware of what you are experiencing at the moment you are experiencing it. You also need to learn how to be centred (this means having a sense of being fully connected with yourself, with others, and what surrounds you), how to be present in the 'here' and 'now', and conscious of knowing what you are doing and why you are doing it.

Therefore training your unconscious mind to help you achieve what you want in your life is a worthwhile investment in time and energy because it will enable you to bring your true passion to the fore, making this the leading force that allows you to succeed as a New Entrepreneur. And how can you start doing that?

Let's begin by seeing what happens to the tiny frogs.

The Story Of The Tiny Frogs

There once was a bunch of tiny frogs who arranged a running competition. The goal was to reach the top of a very tall tower.

A big crowd gathered around the base of the tower to see the race and cheer on the contestants, though none in the crowd really believed that the tiny frogs would ever reach the top.

'It's too tall',' said some in the crowd.

'They aren't strong enough,' said others.

'Or brave enough,' said the rest.

Well, the race began and the frogs set off, leaping and jumping upward. But one by one they collapsed, though a few managed to keep on climbing, higher and higher.

But many in the crowd still doubted that any could reach the top.

'It's too difficult,' they said to each other. 'No one will make it to the top.'

And it looked as though they were right as more and more of the tiny frogs grew too weak to go higher.

But one did continue. Higher and higher and higher he climbed, never thinking of giving up, only intent on reaching the top until with one final effort he was there. He had reached the top.

Naturally, all the other tiny frogs wanted to know how he succeeded when they had failed.

'How did you manage to do that?' they asked. But the winner of the climbing race didn't hear them because he was deaf!

And the moral of this story?

Words have such power that what you hear and read will affect your actions. So, if you listen too much to others, then their negative and pessimistic opinions and thoughts will spoil your dreams and stop you achieving them. This means that if you want to fulfill your dreams you must be *deaf* when people tell you what you can and cannot do. Always think: I can do this!

> ### Action Step
> 1. Think of something you want to achieve. Something that is important for you. Keep it short and simple. For instance, 'I want to enjoy my work more' or 'I want to be present'. Write this down.
>
> 2. Now write alongside the thing you want to achieve, 'I can do this!' and put this on your bathroom mirror so you can read it out aloud every day, morning and night. When you say it, feel it with all your heart.
>
> 3. Believe in what you say and keep working to achieve it! Keep your mind focused on this goal and keep training for success. Keep repeating 'I can do this!' to yourself and out loud too.

Your Notes

_____

_____

_____

_____

_____

Your Unconscious Mind Can't Distinguish Between Fantasy And Reality

It is vital that you understand the nature of your unconscious mind because it's seven times more powerful than your conscious mind. It makes up 88% of your total mind power and therefore exerts an exceptional influence on your everyday existence by filtering your hidden inner thoughts to give you intuition and insights; as well as storing and organising your memories, emotions and beliefs and maintaining and running your body and energy.

This is what happened to those little frogs, who believed what others were saying and so sabotaged their unconscious minds which were unable to distinguish what was real from what was not. They believed that what others were saying was true, and this made them lose their connection with themselves and their dreams and so they failed as a result.

To become a New Entrepreneur you need to learn how to make your unconscious mind work with your conscious mind as a team, and this will allow you to go through life being true to yourself, being congruent, and being happy too. You will become an unstoppable powerhouse able to bring light to any situation. Can you imagine already how different your life would be?

You need to know how to make your unconscious mind support you in achieving what you want. Never underestimate the power of your mind: it's like a lighthouse fully powered which just needs to be plugged in to the right things, to your dreams. Don't stop searching until you are clear about what you want.

These are **10 Rules To Empower Your Unconscious Mind™**:

1. Your unconscious doesn't know what is real, it can't distinguish between physical reality and what you are thinking – if it's in your mind, it's real to it because your unconscious has no sense of humour, takes everything literally and only follows the orders that the conscious mind allows through.

2. It doesn't understand the past or the future, the only thing it knows is the 'now', so all stored experiences are processed as being in the present. This is why it's important to affirm in the present, not in the future.

3. It does not understand negatives. If you say 'I will not lose my job', guess what, you unconscious mind only hears 'I will lose my job'. So, state all affirmations in the positive, removing any suggestion of the negative. For instance, 'I am secure in my job'.

4. The unconscious mind is programmed by repetition, authority, and emotion. So, affirm and visualise with passion and emotional power, seeing what you want to achieve as if it's already real and present now in your life.

5. Your unconscious mind responds with instinct and habit, and this is why changing habits is harder when they become ingrained patterns. Your unconscious mind follows the path of least resistance, working on the principle of least effort. And habits are a shortcut response to a situation. So watch your habits!

6. It stores and represses memories from unresolved negative emotions that then affect your experience now. Take the opportunity to release guilt, fear, anger or depression, by observing when these emotions come along, instead of trying to repress them. Do this, and you can learn how to own these emotions and release them.

7. Your unconscious mind uses symbols and metaphors. Observing and monitoring your dreams, thoughts and the language you use to express your experiences, will give you insights into the way your unconscious mind works. Writing your dreams down will also help you better understand the messages you need to become aware of to understand your own experience.

8. Your unconscious mind takes everything personally, so that as you judge others and project your negative thoughts on to them, you are

in fact doing this to yourself too, like making a photocopy in your own internal system.

9. One of the main roles of your unconscious mind is protection. It wants to help you live a better life, supporting your evolution towards personal growth, love, beauty, truth and fulfillment.

10. Your unconscious mind likes clear, simple, uncluttered and specific instructions that are short, to the point and without ambiguity. Try to say to it what you want in five words or less. For example: *'I want to feel happy now'* instead of *'I want to feel happy when Marc tells me I have done a good job and then...* Your unconscious can't deal with ambiguity, so give it clear orders.

Now that you know yourself better, you can choose freely what matters most to you.

At any point you can choose to be 'this or that'. Knowing what you really want, and what achieving this would mean to you, makes all the difference, so it's worthwhile finding out.

So, like in the little frog's story the deafness of the frog that reached the top prevented the negative voices and influences in the crowd getting into his unconscious mind and affecting his beliefs, you need to use your conscious mind to apply the **10 Rules To Empower Your Unconscious Mind™** to filter what your unconscious mind is hearing. Don't allow anything or anybody to dilute your dreams and the success you can achieve. Successful entrepreneurs spend a lot of effort training their unconscious mind to reach mastery in their lives.

I meet people all the time who live in the future. They like to think that the grass is greener on the other side, so they are always running to get the latest gadget. Their diary is full of activities for the week and it's even fuller during the weekend. They have about them a feeling of restlessness as they try to fill the emptiness they feel inside. They have it all, but they have lost themselves. They are scared to be alone, of not doing something on Saturday night, of not being invited to the next 'great' event, of being left behind, of being forgotten.

But happiness can only be experienced in the present and this should be your goal. As your unconscious mind only understands the present, the more in the 'here' and 'now' you are able to be, the easier it will be for you to take the right decisions and for you to be happy with your life and 'what it is'.

To get through this, you may need to accept a feeling of temporary loneliness and discomfort, but this is part of the process and it's normal.

This is the quest you must take on, if ultimately what you want is to feel free, really free to live your life on your terms, with all its ups and downs. Life is not a straight line, you do not drive on a motorway with no exits or junctions, rather your route takes you on a journey of twisted and curvy roads.

When you live in the present, you already feel happy and successful with whatever you own and have achieved. You are able to accept where you are right now at the same time as having clear goals about what you want next; savouring the moment for what it is, being grateful to feel alive and with so many opportunities ahead of you. Every day is just a new beginning which allows you to become whoever you are meant to be. Carpe Diem!

Mistakes Are Not Failures, Just New Opportunities

How important are your beliefs? If you were able to believe, even for a second, that everything that has happened in your life is exactly as it is supposed to be, that the family you were born into was selected to help you become who you are today... that nothing has happened by accident but is part of your story that is still unfolding ahead of you. If you were able to believe this, even for a second, you will perceive your whole life up to now with a different perspective.

And if you could believe this, then how differently would you feel about your life, your experiences, your challenges, the moments that you wished all was so different?

Without contrast in your life it is hard to know what is good or bad, what to choose and what not. Without options all the world looks flat, with no landmarks to head for, and any direction in which you go being but an arbitrary choice. And would you want to leave your choices to luck?

We have looked at 'luck' as something that you create, not something that just happens by accident and without any intervention on your part.

So, believing that something can happen in your life increases the probabilities of making it happen. Remember that your unconscious mind can't distinguish between what is real and what is not. If you believe something, then that thought will be treated as real and help you make it happen. So, keep focused on your goals – relying on winning the lottery is not a realistic route to make your dreams come true – and don't give up at the first upset.

Life will test you, so make sure you know what you want: the reward is immense when you arrive at your new destination, even though this often turns out to be somewhere different from where you had originally planned. As a bonus you will have grown up on the journey and feel much more powerful and resilient, being well prepared to enjoy the results and better suited to take on a bigger challenge next.

Have you ever tried to do something a thousand times in the same way, just getting the same poor results? This is what most people do because it's easier than trying to do one thing a thousand different ways, each of which might give you a new result.

Your unconscious mind likes repetition, so the more you do the same thing, the more important your unconscious mind considers this thing to be, and so it learns faster and becomes ever better at doing it. Great if this is what you want, bad if it isn't.

I hope that by now you already have an idea of what you can do differently.

Have you ever wanted to know exactly how things will turn out before taking a decision or a risk? Don't.

Instead, stop being a control freak, get engaged with your life, go through the discomfort of finding out who you truly are and what you want to create. Even if you don't like what you find, the good news is that as a human being you can easily learn new things and so have the power to change what you put your mind into. Yes, really. Your unconscious mind will believe whatever you believe, so feed it wisely. Train your mind for success. Success is a decision.

Beware... Others Will Love To Tell You How To Live Your Life, Especially Those Who Are Too Scared To Live Theirs

Have you ever suggested to others what to do with their life? Giving them ideas and suggestions from your heart, because you care, because you think you understand their situation, because you have experienced similar things, because after all you have more experience, because, because...?

Almost certainly yes.

And guess what? Others are doing the same to you: your parents, your friends, the TV, the media, your teachers, everybody thinks they have the right to give you their opinion, even when you haven't asked for it!

So, make sure you are discerning about who you listen to, after all it's your life and you are the only expert on it! Remember, your unconscious mind will believe whatever you choose to believe.

You hear things like: 'Why don't you do this?' or, 'This works for me, surely it will work for you too?' or even worse, 'That won't work so there's no point trying'. All these phrases are given with the best of intentions but have a powerful impact on your life if you don't stand up for yourself and become clear about what is important for you.

What do *you* want? It's one of the most important questions, and you and only you can find the right answer for you. Yet most adults go from one thing to another without having a clue of what they really want. So, you spend years studying and planning your career, but how long have you spent planning your life as a whole?

That's right, you haven't.

Then you ask yourself: how did my life turn out to be this way? Every area of your life – from your profession, your job, your relationships, your friendships, your holiday, your health, everything without exception requires careful planning, a clear vision and purpose, and it's something you've never done.

That's like having other people choose pieces from lots of different jigsaw puzzles and then suddenly bring them together to make something that's called – Your Life.

Don't leave any piece for others to choose, because every decision matters!

There Is No Traced Path For You To Follow ... You Have To Create YOUR Own

Nobody apart from you has an answer to what will next happen in your life, because you are on a continual quest throughout your whole existence. So, you choose a path today and set out along it, only for something unexpected to happen tomorrow, but rather than going back to the start as so many do, wouldn't it be better to ask yourself some powerful questions that will help you move forwards from where you are?

Questions like: 'Am I on the right path in the first place?' 'Is this what I want to have or experience in my life right now?' 'How do I feel about this aspect of my life?' 'Is there something I would like to be different about my life?'

Be like a hyperactive Sherlock Holmes searching for clues and answers, and never stop asking those questions.

You Already Know What Life Has To Offer If You Have The Courage To Go After It

Deep down, you have dreams, ideas about things you would like to explore, but then the self-doubt creeps in, the internal voices start, and you take detours based on what others think. All these obstacles stop you from taking action and will keep you stuck where you are if you are not careful. Remember the story of the little frogs, when others were telling them that they would never succeed?

Can you remember the times when you wanted to be a film star, a scientist winning the Nobel Prize, a writer that made kids laugh? Do you remember your childhood heroes and the qualities you admired in them? Who were your role models then?

More importantly, who are your role models today? The people you consider worth listening to, the ones you want to follow, and the ones you would love to meet face to face to ask for advice.

One of the important things to realise is that, whoever you spend your time with, you become. If you surround yourself with people who are always complaining, have no money, have no ambitions, or have no dreams, then this is who you will become.

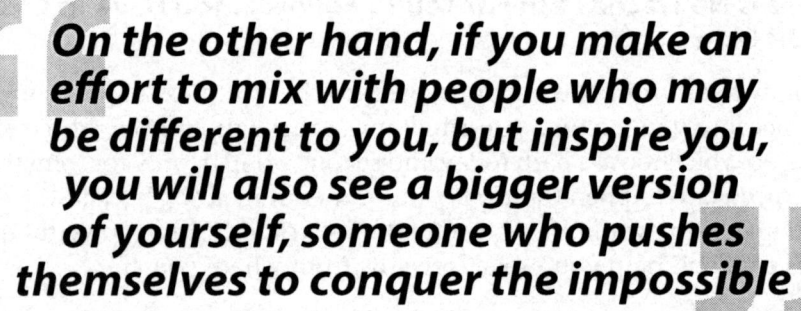

On the other hand, if you make an effort to mix with people who may be different to you, but inspire you, you will also see a bigger version of yourself, someone who pushes themselves to conquer the impossible

And of course, the good news is that you can choose who to spend your time with and who to mix with.

Don't Spend Major Time With Minor People

If there are people in your life who continually disappoint you, break promises, stamp on your dreams, are too judgmental, have different values or don't watch your back during difficult times... then they are not friends.

But to have a friend, you need to be a friend.

Sometimes in life as you grow, your friends will either grow with you or go.

So, surround yourself with people who reflect your values, goals, interests and lifestyle.

When I think of any of my successes, I am thankful to God from whom all blessings flow, and to my family and friends who enrich my life.

Over the years, my phone book has changed because I've changed, for the better. At first, you think you're going to be alone, but after a while, new people show up in your life who will make it all so much sweeter and easier to endure.

Remember That Old Saying

'Birds of a feather flock together'. So, if you're an Eagle, don't hang around with Chickens because chickens can't fly!'

> **Exercise 10**
>
> 1. What is this story telling you?
>
> 2. Make a list of the people, currently in your life, who it's about time you 'let go'.

Your Notes

....

....

....

....

....

N.B. There are more bonus exercises to help you with this section online at: **www.maitebaron.com/resourcepack**

Today the internet and YouTube give you access to view, read and listen to people who are changing the world and to those who are leaders in their different disciplines or heroes across all times and cultures. Today, you can choose to use your time to learn, to get inspired, to grow, or just to waste it playing games.

Yet many people prefer to do a bit of this and a bit of that, filling their head with noise and wasting their time. The net result is that they end up with little purpose or direction for their actions, and without becoming a better human being their life just drifts away.

And by the way, today there is no longer any excuse for not achieving greatness, whoever you are; you are just perfectly positioned to make it happen. If you are reading this book, the likelihood is that you are fortunate enough to live in a civilised country where you can obtain as much education as anybody else if you have access to a computer. So stop the nonsense.

> **Action Step**
>
> Ask yourself:
>
> 1. Which role do I want to play in life?
>
> 2. Who would I like to become?
>
> 3. What do I need to do to make this happen?

This will help you to start creating a plan for your life because it's something that is far too precious to leave up to others, or to chance, or to external circumstances, with no purpose or direction.

If you are one of those professionals who always wanted to work in another country, get yourself together, get up the courage, and go!

The other day I overheard a conversation on a plane between a father and his son. The father would have been over 75 and the son about 55. The son said to his father that he had always wanted to live in the Swiss Alps because he loved skiing, being in the open air and enjoying the outdoors, but that as all his friends were in London it was easier to carry on with his life as it was.

I thought to myself? What is this guy waiting for? He's certainly not a spring chicken. What needs to happen for him to get the courage to go and live his life as he wants and dreams?

Today, with the technology available to every one of us, distance doesn't really exist. Yes, he may need to adapt how he works, but things far more complicated than this have been accomplished with a bit of planning.

The Courage To Love

I believe that there is nothing that requires more courage than being in love, and I don't mean a fling or staying with somebody because you can't be alone.

To fall in love with someone you cherish every day, to feel grateful for waking up and going to bed with this person whose presence makes you smile day after day; the special person with whom you can truly be yourself; the one who gets your bad jokes; the one you don't need to talk to in order to have a conversation; the one who, when they look at you, makes you feel the sun inside even when it's cold and rainy outside. Do you know what I'm talking about?

This is the one, who knows you well, believes in you and pushes you out of your comfort zone for you to grow and to reach your full potential. This is the one who pushes you to break free from your inner prison walls.

I hope you are not the one that once fell in love, but never told the other because you were scared of rejection, and have since then settled with somebody else but are living your life without love and passion.

There is nothing in life that makes you feel more alive than being permanently in love, and the best is that when you feel like this, you feel alive in every area of your life, your friendships, your work, your hobbies. However, in order to fall in love with another and with your life, you need to love yourself first. And this is an alien concept for lot of people.

As you start your journey to becoming a New Entrepreneur, share your thoughts and dreams with your loved ones. It's crucial you bring them on board, for as you well know, nobody can make it alone!

Sharing Is Caring

You will notice throughout this book that I have highlighted some of the key learning in bite-size quotes that you can share on Facebook, LinkedIn, or Twitter really easily. Next to the most 'tweet-able' quotes you will see this symbol:

 #CorporateEscape

You can also recommend this book by sharing this link:

www.maitebaron.com/corporateescapebook

Why does this matter? Because, by helping others you will be helping yourself too. It's easier to recommend a book to people you want to be on the same page with, rather than attempting to make them understand what you are trying to say out of the blue. When you need to make a point that you may find difficult, you can refer to a section by saying: 'Do you remember in the Corporate Escape book about the importance of following your passion? Well this is what I feel I need to do now...'

The Path Is Not Straight, Be Ready To Travel For A While And Don't Forget To Bring Your Dreams Along

Every month I visit my mother-in-law who is in a care home and each time I go I have a mixture of feelings: curiosity about all the residents' life stories; a sense of how quickly life goes and that each day counts; the wonder of how many unsung songs are there, full of lost dreams; and how much guilt and sadness there is for things done or undone. All in front of me to witness and to not forget.

So, whatever you need the courage for, start building it today, stretch yourself doing things that feel challenging, step by step, build the muscle... all this will be well worth the effort when the time comes to look back at your life. You will be able to say: 'I have no regrets', 'I committed mistakes but I felt alive', 'I lived, I loved, I made a difference to others with my work, and as a result I made the world a better place'. Well, if you want this to be true for you, then you need to start today.

After all you are an Eagle, the Leader of your life, opening your wings to expand your flight and lead yourself forward.

Key Ideas To Take Away

1. Reality doesn't exist. You see the world not as it is, but as you are. When you grow and expand your thinking, the world around you will look and feel different as if you are suddenly walking without all those filters on your glasses. Everything will look brighter, including the present and your future.

2. Don't try to fake it by trying to copy someone else. Others will feel the falseness. Set your sights on being the perfect 'you', not an imperfect copy of somebody else.

3. Security is a fallacy. Conformity is a recipe for mediocrity, and the illusion of stability makes you a prisoner of your own life. Be clear about what you want, what you stand for and what matters to you, and forget the rest.

4. At any given moment you are free to believe whatever you want. Your unconscious mind can't differentiate between what is real and what is not, so use this to your advantage by focusing only on what you want to create and attract. Your unconscious mind is your ally, so learn to speak its language by practicing the **10 Rules To Empower Your Unconscious Mind™** and treat it with respect – it's a precious partner.

5. Even though others gave you a path to follow from the moment you were born, remember that in order to own your life you need to create your own!

6. By now you know that in order to become a New Entrepreneur you need to shift your thinking and your mindset, and as a result your whole world will shift with you.

Your journey to become a New Entrepreneur has started!

Your Notes

In Chapter 4, you will learn…

How to identify where you are right now and the challenges and opportunities that this brings to your life, in both the short and long term. Life is about choices, and you need to have a bigger vision for your life so that it is about more than just money. You need to understand the relationship between love, wealth and success and why without love in your life all else will feel worthless. And that being true to yourself, your values and being your real self is the key to finding real love. After all, the quality of your interactions with others comes from the heart not from your mind. You will also come to know more about your mind, **The 4 Emotional Mirrors Of The Brain™**, and the relationship between **The 7 CEOs Who Run Your Mind™**. So you can live a life where there is balance between the decisions taken by your mind, your heart and your soul.

In this chapter we will explore **The *SUPER* – Generation™** and **The *SUPER* + Generation™** and what you can do to start taking control of your life by making your values, together with your mission, your driving force.

Chapter 4

Life Is About Choices

You Are Today Exactly Where You Planned To Be, Aren't You?

Imagine for a moment that you are sitting and thinking about your life, your dreams and plans, and how your life has unfolded. Are you where you planned to be? Of course, this question only makes sense if you had a plan in the first place.

Maybe you're not sure, perhaps it's more like a nagging feeling that there must be more to life, that you are a bit stuck in a rut. This feeling of routine and monotony is starting to get under your skin. You want to do something about it, but you don't know what.

Never allow confusion to stop you; clarity can only come from starting to move in one direction and then making adjustments as you progress. It is like driving on a route you don't know. At some point you discover you're lost, stop for a moment and then keep changing direction until you find the right way.

That is of course until next time. So, yes... there will be more confusion and more exploration as you progress through life and you will need to find new clarity and a new way forward.

This is life, so it's better to understand and accept it and just keep moving. Obviously having a map to get where you are going can give you clarity. Just make sure you choose the map that takes you where *you* want to go.

> **Life is not about security, conformity, or stability, its about being able to find balance in the middle of change & chaos #CorporateEscape**

Until now, everybody else has given you a map that puts you on a path that may be right for them but not you. You have heard this loads of times: 'If you go to university you'll have a guaranteed job or career for life.' 'If you get married young you will be settled.' You believed it and you followed their advice and today you are stuffed, or perhaps not yet. In any case, this could have been true 20 or so years ago, but not any longer.

You already know by now that there is no such thing as a job or career for life, and if you still hold this belief then you'd better erase it from your mind right now, before it's too late. Now it's time to start making better choices for yourself.

> **Life's about constant evolution, not the perpetuation of the old. The goal is to keep learning, independently of your work! #CorporateEscape**

So Where Are You Now?

Whatever the decisions and choices you have made in your life, you've probably always thought they were for the best at the time... though not necessarily afterwards. Irrespective of that, all of those decisions that you have made have brought you to the place you are now.

So, let's consider where that is and some of the options that are now available to you.

Here are the four scenarios that most professionals typically find themselves in. Your exact situation might not be exactly as described here, but there will certainly be features you can relate to.

Scenario 1: Unfulfilled, Burned-out And Disillusioned

You're in your 40s – although I'm seeing many more in their mid-30s who are already falling into this group, and I suspect that soon I will be seeing many more.

You went to university and studied for a degree or professional qualification, after which you thought you were set for a lifelong career.

But now, some 15 or 20 years down the road, all is not going to plan. For starters, despite your relative success to date, you don't want to spend the next two or three decades in the same career or job, especially as you can see that progression has become synonymous with over-work, high levels of stress, poor health, little free time, and the high probability of a divorce or a failed relationship. You certainly see this happening to others. It's not an attractive option or one that feels right for you any longer.

If you are in this group, you're looking for an alternative and you have two main choices:

1. Change nothing and just soldier on until redundancy or some other peril of corporate life overwhelms you. Just changing jobs for more of the same is not going to fix this situation.

2. Or, you could ask yourself: 'What do I really want out of my life? Who do I want to become? Do I want to have a life of conformity and mediocrity, or do I want to create a life that is fulfilling and meaningful to myself and others?' If you do, then something important needs to change and it has to change soon.

In this group I see professionals who want to leave the 'traditional' working path and create something new that leverages their skills and knowledge in a completely different way. I see executives leaving large corporations to become CEOs of smaller companies, not only to progress up the career ladder but also to improve their life/work balance.

I also see executives and managers who are desperate to leave the corporate world and are looking for an alternative, often wanting to start their own business, even though they are not sure what this might look like. There are also more and more couples, bringing together their complementary skills to create a lifestyle business. Are any of these people potentially you?

Scenario 2: Between Jobs Or Being Made Redundant

No matter how carefully you have planned your career, you already know that job security is something that only happened in the past. And with many companies now cutting corners wherever they can so as to stay profitable, redundancy is an increasingly first-choice method of cost cutting, certainly before reducing bonuses!

Redundancy is a traumatic experience for anyone, particularly if you thought your career was going well. If this happens, then often the initial response is, of course, to spend days sending off CVs, phoning recruitment agencies and chasing job leads. But the reality is that the world of employment is changing significantly. Big employers are being squeezed and they no longer want to have long-term professionals on their payroll.

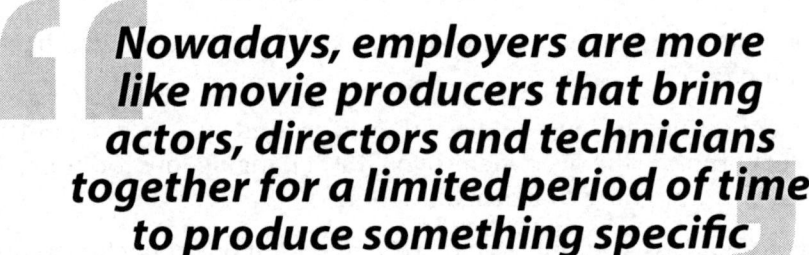

> *Nowadays, employers are more like movie producers that bring actors, directors and technicians together for a limited period of time to produce something specific*

If you want to play this game, you need to be someone specialised with valuable and appropriate skills and knowledge to offer. After all, you wouldn't cast Mr Bean as the lead in a movie like The King's Speech, would you? If you don't get it right and become too much of a generalist, then there's a high probability of ending up with a role in the next scenario.

Scenario 3: Your Career Options Are Shrinking

If you do find yourself stuck in a job that's tolerable as opposed to stimulating, you can't allow yourself to become complacent. I'm seeing an increasing number of highly skilled professionals and executives who are being affected by one or more of the drivers of employment change, for example: globalisation, the technology squeeze, outsourcing, the credit crunch... and who knows what else. So, it's important to be aware that as jobs become more and more systemised and automated, just updating your skill set and your experience, or maintaining your position, is not necessarily going to keep you in the workplace.

If you want to stay in demand, you have to do more than just tick boxes. As Einstein put it:

'It is not so very important for a person to learn facts. For that he does not really need a college. He can learn them from books. The value of an education in a liberal arts college is not the learning of many facts but the training of the mind to think something that cannot be learned from textbooks.'

Therefore it's imperative to learn more than just new skills – you need to be able to make fundamental shifts in your attitudes, your beliefs and your paradigms to create the biggest difference in your life: you need a new mindset (but more on this later).

It's the professionals who're responsive to change and flexible in their thinking who will continue to progress #CorporateEscape

> **Those who remain bound by habitual thinking will be permanently relegated to lower-grade jobs, earning the minimum wage #CorporateEscape**

And I'm pretty sure that this is not what you are looking for. But being willing to challenge your own sense of identity requires courage, discipline and willpower, and often professional support. But I guarantee it's worthwhile, because learning how to become more agile in your approach to change is a long-term skill that will serve you well, whatever comes your way.

Scenario 4: Self-Employed But Squeezed

This last scenario applies to those who are self-employed, such as freelancers, consultants and those who own small businesses either through choice or as a 'no alternative' solution.

With the explosion of the internet and increasing globalisation, the way we do business now is rapidly changing. As a result, many businesses are struggling to cope with the unfamiliar challenges.

For example, with the increasing popularity of online shopping, business location is far less important than it used to be. So, with a well-crafted website, you can reach potential clients all over the world, and engage them with new marketing tools, such as social media. The point here is that...

> **... regardless of your industry and target audience, businesses need to be flexible in their thinking and willing to let go of out-dated approaches that no longer get results**

You don't necessarily need to change 'what' you do – but rather the way you think and how you do it, since you will need not only an up-to-date business model but also the right focus and mindset so you can move from having the mentality of an employee to that of a New Entrepreneur.

Who Are You To Disagree, Anyway?

There is always somebody that believes they have more life experience than you, when in reality they just have more years under their belt, not more experiences. Their life has been practically the same for ages! The same job, the same partner, the same holiday, same restaurants, same friends. So, what about you? Is your life one of many experiences, or just a few endlessly repeated? If that's the case, then you have an opportunity now to create new ones, ones that feel right for you, at this moment in your life.

I can't stand it when people say: 'You will not know until you do it.' And while this may apply sometimes, it's far from a universal truth because there are things that you don't need to do to know that they aren't what you want!

When I dropped out of my psychology degree after two years, I had enough experience of my teachers and peers to know that I was in the wrong place and that if I spent five years of my life doing what my teachers had done and still had as little understanding about real people as they did, what would be the point? I felt more whole and balanced as an 18-year-old woman then, even with all the ups and downs that come with that age, than any of those 30- and 40-year-old academics around me.

At least I knew who I was.

Since then, I've always been wary of any scientific approaches to life. Science is good as far as it goes, but it can forget to include the human dimension that makes us who we are.

Let's have a look at this old story about the two wolves...

A Story Of Two Wolves

An old Cherokee is teaching his grandson about life.

'A fight is going on inside me,' he says to the boy, 'and it is a terrible fight between two wolves. One of them is evil – full of anger, envy, sorrow, regret, greed, arrogance, self-pity, guilt, resentment, fear, inferiority, lies, false pride and ego.'

'But the other is good. He is full of joy, peace, love, hope, serenity, humility, kindness, benevolence, empathy, generosity, truth, compassion, and faith.'

'This same fight is going on inside you – and inside every other person, too.'

The grandson thought about this for a minute and then asked his grandfather: 'Which wolf will win?'

The old Cherokee replied: 'The one you feed.'

Exercise 11

1. Which wolf inside you is the one you feed most?
2. How does feeding this wolf affect your life?
3. Where would you like to put your focus of attention instead?
4. How would your life be different as a result, if you did this?

Your Notes

_____

_____

_____

_____

_____

> *Yes you have emotions. They are a gift to be mastered and conquered so you can ride your mind instead of your mind riding you #CorporateEscape*

There Is More To Life Than Money

You Have Done As You Were Told, But Something Is Still Missing

Your life is so busy and complex that there is hardly any 'you' time.

You care about everybody, but who cares about you? Whatever life brings your way, there is a constant pattern, you seem always to come last and seem to 'disappear' a little from view each day.

You can't carry on like this because you just can't give to others what you don't have, by which I mean that if you feel exhausted you can't give energy; if you feel depleted you can't really care. Everything that you then do becomes just another task on your endless 'to do' list. You need to recharge your batteries first in order to be able to provide for others afterwards.

This means that thinking about you is not selfish, but actually a matter of personal responsibility. It is also an important skill if you are to become a successful (and we will review what success is later on) New Entrepreneur.

And this applies to every area of your life. If you do a job you hate, you impact negatively on every person you interact with because you can't offer an enjoyable and amazing experience to others if you are not having this amazing experience yourself first.

Have you ever gone out for a meal wanting to feel chilled out and just be taken care of? But the waiter takes ages to come for your order, the food is not quite what you expected, you need to mention that the frites are missing and that you would like some ketchup and mustard, and then eventually one of these arrives but not the other. And when the other does, you've already finished you meal. Then, when you want to leave the waiter and bill are nowhere to be seen.

So, you feel disappointed with the whole experience; the relationship between the quality of the food, your experience overall and the price you paid for the meal somehow just don't match. You say to yourself that next time you will go somewhere else.

And then, restaurants complain about lack of customers!

The truth is that the waiter was tired and didn't care. He is doing the job just to earn some money, waiting is clearly not his life dream and he can't wait to get out of there. So, even though none of this was spoken, his dissatisfaction was felt in every interaction with you and affected your whole experience.

I'm fed up with poor service, but unfortunately, scenarios like this are all too common in so many contexts... professionally and personally.

When you do something without putting your heart in it, then it comes across as pointless and meaningless.

If you are doing something you don't love, take responsibility and do something about it. Today there are more employment options than in any other generation before, so make the most of them. Yes, I know that what you read in the news and hear in the TV is the very opposite, that unemployment is growing; and how thousands of jobs are being lost every day and so on. But if you are willing to open your mind and widen your horizons then you will discover an amazing sea of opportunities that were not available before.

Embrace technology and the wide open market that the internet offers to each one of us and you will start noticing doors opening all the way around you. I'm not saying that everything is rosy and easy, what I believe is that the parameters of the working world have moved and new ones are being defined. That means you can even work internationally without ever leaving your desk, or home. Just a few years ago, this was not possible, and to me this is great news.

Who Told You That Life Was About Enjoyment And Fulfillment?

Since you were a child, you saw adults struggling, complaining about their lives and feeling dissatisfied with their lot. You kept hearing that they need to endure their job because it paid the bills, and that anyone was lucky to have a job at all, and that life was all about being an adult and responsible, which meant there was no opportunity for enjoyment, fulfillment and fun.

Unfortunately you believed them. This may have been true during the agricultural and industrial revolutions and for much of the 20th Century, but for God's sake, we are now in the 21st Century and this is no longer true.

> **Make a living doing what you love. Turn your passion into a business that will create the fulfilling lifestyle you want #CorporateEscape** 🐦

Again nobody can tell you what you can or can't do with your life, that is your choice alone, you just need to learn how to make better decisions about it, and that's something you'll learn later. So for now, you only need to find out *what* you want do. The *how* will come later.

So, Why Aren't You Happy?

Right now you don't know whether to stay in your job or to leave and follow your dreams. There are so many unanswered questions buzzing around in your head.

What would happen if you took the wrong path again? What if it doesn't work and you leave your job and you can't make ends meet? What will others say? Wouldn't this be selfish of you to put all at risk to follow your dreams?

Then others might say to you: 'What are you complaining about? You have it all. How can you be so selfish and ungrateful?'

But that's not the reality you're experiencing, and given their thoughts, it's getting harder and harder to relate to your friends any longer, because they are happy to perpetuate their unfulfilling existences while you are not.

No one seems to understand your world.

You even feel a fraud because you could just keep going up your career ladder. Most people around you are feeling much the same, but you know this is not what you want.

So why can't you just switch off that annoying little voice inside your head that keeps telling you: 'You need to do something about this. You can't stay like this forever wasting your talents.'

Our Lives In Money

A well-known speaker began his seminar by holding up a $100 note to a room of 200 people.

'Who would like this $100 note?' he asked.

Everyone's hand went up.

'Then I will give this $100 to one of you here, but first, let me do this.'

He proceeded to crumple the $100 note up and then held it up.

'Who still wants this?' he asked.

All hands went up once more.

'Well,' said the speaker, 'would you still want it if I did this?' and he dropped the bill and ground it into the floor with his shoe before picking up the now crumpled and dirty note.

'Now who still wants it?'

Still the hands went into the air.

'My friends, we have all learned a very valuable lesson,' said the speaker, 'no matter what I did to the money, you still wanted it because it did not decrease in value. It is still worth $100.'

And The Moral Of This Story?

Many times in our lives, we are dropped, crumpled, and ground into the dirt by the decisions we make and the circumstances that come our way. We feel as though we are worthless. But no matter what has happened or what will happen, you will never lose your value. Dirty or clean, crumpled or finely creased, you are still priceless… and especially to those who love you. The worth of our lives comes not in what we do or whom we know, but in who we are.

Exercise 12

1. What is this story telling you? What do you learn from it?

2. Until now, how have you been measuring your value?

3. How can you expand the concept of value and what is worth looking at?

Your Notes

You Need A Bigger Vision For Your Life

You have seen what happens when you allow things just to happen without having clear intention or clarity of direction. But today, right now, you can create a new vision for your life, a destination that motivates and excites you, and this applies to every area of your life.

Let's have a look at how.

It's helpful to know what is your own reality, because by knowing that you can be empowered to take action. Reply to each of these questions honestly, because while you can kid others, what's the point of kidding yourself!

Do you know what you want to experience more of at work?	Yes / No
Are you happy with your working life and with the challenges and the opportunities it brings you?	Yes / No
Are you looking forward to going to work on Monday with excitement and joy?	Yes / No
Are you clear about what you want to experience on a daily basis, on a weekly basis, or at least on a monthly basis?	Yes / No
Does your working reality provide you with personal, emotional, financial and spiritual fulfillment? Or with an opportunity for ongoing learning?	Yes / No
Do you feel passionate about what you do and with whom you work?	Yes / No

Your Notes

If you answered 'No' to more than one question, then *now* is the time to do something about this and take control of your working life. Why? Because, if it doesn't give you a sense of fulfillment then your work is draining away your energy, which means you are not doing your best or standing out from the crowd, and in return your clients or customers are not having the amazing experience that they deserve to have.

If you are not learning new skills, you are putting yourself in a vulnerable position and are more at risk of becoming unmarketable even before you realise it. If you are not passionate about what you do, then you are not willing to put in the extra effort that is necessary and to go the extra mile that elevates an ordinary experience into an extraordinary one. Sooner or later, this will become evident to the rest of the world.

Exercise 13

What applies to your work life also applies to your personal life, so:

1. What are the three words you would like to use to describe the amazing relationship you always dreamed of?
2. Is this how you would describe your current relationship?

Your Notes

If you answered 'No' to Question 2 above, *now* is the time to do something about it. Why?

Because unless it feels as though you have a nurturing, passionate and exciting relationship then you are keeping yourself away from one you could have, and you will keep holding back just for the sake of having someone next to you.

I talk from experience, and so I know there is nothing more painful then feeling alone while being in a relationship, when you feel that somehow by accident you have just landed there in a place that was never meant to be.

After my divorce, I was very clear that I would rather be alone than in a mediocre relationship. I could cope with living by myself but not lying to myself about believing that something was there when it wasn't. Another big lesson was to understand that to make a great relationship work you need two people who want the same thing and are looking in the same direction.

> **A relationship must have active commitment else you'll overcompensate for what's missing & you can't do that forever #CorporateEscape**

So, be honest with yourself and face what needs to be faced. When you look fear in the face, its strength seems to vanish. When you stop feeding it, it dies on its own. It's scary at the beginning, especially if you have lived together for so long, but when you become aware that this is not a healthy relationship, in fact it's toxic, then you are left with no other choice than to either work it out or leave.

Quite surprisingly, when many people talk to me about their relationships, strangers out of the blue or clients out of context, they ask: 'If you don't have any intimacy in your relationship is this a reason for you to leave?'

This is not for me to say but for you to ask yourself how important is this for you? How do you feel when you are intimate with the person you love? How do you feel when there is no proximity for weeks or months? What is the impact on your self-esteem? How do you see yourself in the world around you? And how do you envisage your future with this person? And in general in your life?

For me it is clear, in a loving relationship there must be intimacy, in fact, I can't imagine not wanting to be intimate with the person I love. Without intimacy a relationship becomes just a friendship, period. Is this what you want? If the answer is no, then stop kidding yourself and everybody else and get your act together to face this truth. Life is short; stop wasting such an amazing time.

Don't ever underestimate the things you want to experience in your daily life. Do you want to have more time to read, or to walk in the park? To stroll without hurrying so you can smell the flowers on your way to work? To enjoy a conversation with your friends without being rushed, just being with them without time mattering at all?

Your Notes

N.B. There are more bonus exercises for this section in your worksheets pack online. Go to: **www.maitebaron.com/resourcepack**

You may have noticed that throughout the book I refer to Work, Leadership and Love nearly simultaneously. My belief is that unless you are in love, unless love is present in your life in one form or another, the choices you will make in your life and your priorities will be based too much on others' values and beliefs and be mostly materialistic which will require you to work harder, longer hours, just for more money.

Love brings a different perspective and other priorities, especially if you already have failed relationships in the past. When you choose from your heart, the quality of your decisions changes radically. What matters for you, your most important values, must be present in your life and you will not accept any shortcuts.

This is very important because others will try to pull you to live their values. I see this all the time when working with corporate clients who expect you to be available 24/7. Nowadays, I will not accept any contract with this expectation because I have a professional life and a personal life, both of which are important to me, and I believe I can have both successfully working in balance.

Also, working with associates who have lifestyle habits that don't fit with my values and priorities can be toxic. For instance, they are willing to work fourteen hours a day, damaging their health and their relationships, then expect that if you work with them you should do the same.

Or, when working with very demanding clients for whom work is the only thing in their lives and they expect you to join their club. I had two relationships in a row with workaholics... and life became meaningless. So make sure you live your life based on your values.

Let me show you how this all relates together with another story...

Three Guests

A woman came out of her house and saw three old men with long white beards sitting in her front yard. She did not recognise them and said: 'I don't think I know you, but you must be hungry. Please come in and have something to eat.'

'Is the man of the house at home?' asked the three together.

'No, he is not,' she replied.

'Then we cannot come in,' said the three.

In the evening when her husband came home, she told him what had happened.

'Go and tell them I'm home,' he said, 'and invite them in!'

This the woman did.

'We do not go into a house together,' replied the three.

'Why is that?' asked the woman.

One of the old men pointed to another: 'His name is Wealth,' he said. He pointed at the other: 'and he is Success, while I am Love.'

'Now go inside and discuss with your husband which one of us you want to enter your home.'

The woman went in and told her husband what she had been told.

Her husband was overjoyed. 'How wonderful!' he cried. 'Let us invite in Wealth so he might fill our home with prosperity.'

But his wife disagreed.

'My dear,' she said, 'why don't we invite in Success, as success can lead us to wealth so that we may have both.'

Their daughter-in-law, who had been listening from a corner of the room, jumped up and said: 'Would it not be better to invite in Love because then our home will be filled with love!'

'Let us heed our daughter-in-law's advice,' said the husband to his wife. 'Go out and invite Love to be our guest.'

The woman went outside and said: 'We have chosen and wish Love to be our guest.'

Love got up and started walking toward the house. The other two also got up and followed him. Surprised, the woman said to Wealth and Success: 'I only invited Love. Why are you coming too?'

The three replied together: 'If you had invited Wealth or Success, the other two of us would've stayed outside, but since you invited Love, wherever he goes, we go with him.'

And the moral of this story?

Wherever there is Love, there is also Wealth and Success!

> **Exercise 14**
> 1. Which of these guests do you invite most and least into your life?
> 2. How does this story relate to your life and the choices you have made so far?
> 3. What changes would you like to create in this new phase of your life?

Your Notes

....

....

....

....

If right now you are not in a relationship then begin the process of bringing love into your life by taking good care of yourself. This is important because if your habits are toxic you will attract those with other toxic habits.

Start noticing all the different areas of your life where love is already present: your family, your friends, your dog and nature. Love is around you in so many ways!

So, don't feel bad if you are not in an intimate relationship right now. What you need to ask yourself is: Do I want a personal relationship? If the answer is yes, then work out what you need to do and to stop doing, to make this happen. Becoming a New Entrepreneur will help you attract love into your life because when you are connected with your values and driven by your passion, you become attractive to others who want to share what you have.

I worked once with a successful career woman who was depressed because everybody else was telling her that she needed to be in a relationship and this was not happening. When we looked at her diary it came clear that 1. she had no time for a relationship; and 2. she didn't want to make any adjustments to her current lifestyle and overloaded diary.

Suddenly, she realised that she didn't have any relationship because this was not a priority for her at this moment in time. Money and climbing the career ladder were her two main drivers.

Whatever you decide to do, is up to you. What matters is that whatever you choose is based on your values, priorities and choices and not somebody else's.

Know what you want, you know what happens
It's time to take control of your life

You need to become aware of what your life really consists of, not just the things you do while on autopilot, but also the things you do because they energise you and because they make you feel good about yourself, people or life.

What is your life about? Let's start with the little things first.

What are you voting for everyday of your life? By this I mean, how do you spend your time, your energy, your money on a daily basis? Everything you do has an impact on your life, on the lives of others, on your business, on the environment and on the planet. You may think I'm nuts, but it's a fact that's how it is. Let me give you an example.

The other day I was in Canary Wharf in London and had some time to sit in the sunshine. There was long queue outside Starbucks with people waiting ten minutes at least to get their latte, or mocha, or cappuccino, whatever they were so keen to get hold of.

Observing the people in the queue, I could see that most of them were completely absent from the moment, just doing what they did every day, perhaps even more than once.

Were they there because they love their coffee so much? Or were they there because it was an excuse to leave work for a while and feel alive? Were they there because they connect with the mission and values of Starbucks and want to make sure their custom keeps the business going?

Every time you buy something from a specific company or business you are voting for them to exist and your actions have a ripple effect. When you match your values with your actions, then you start living a very different kind of existence.

Becoming aware of what you do is the first step to making conscious choices, and by ensuring this becomes a habit, you take control of your life, in every area, one step at the time.

Look at the things you do in your life that don't give you happiness, pleasure or any feel-good factor, the tedious things you do that don't bring you joy.

Exercise 15

Write the first answer that comes into your mind to these questions:

1. What do you need to stop doing right now?
2. What do you want to do more of in your life?
3. What do you want to do less of in your life?
4. And, what are you going to do about it?

Your Notes

Action Step

Commitment starts when you say to someone else what you are going to do.

You can download the 'Today I take control of my life' declaration from

www.maitebaron.com/resourcepack

and post your results in our Facebook page or

 "@maitebaron Today I have committed to take control of my life#CorporateEscape"

It makes a great deal of difference when you make a commitment and it's shared with others; without that it's all too easy to put your own targets and goals to one side and do nothing about them.

Be clear about what you stand for

The easiest way to live a life of congruency, feeling good about yourself and with the world around you, is to live by honouring your values. You may say, 'great, that sounds easy enough', but if it were, why are so few people living like this?

Unfortunately, it's because most people choose poor role-models, few of whom exhibit worthwhile qualities. All too readily, many are seduced by bling, or a 'particular' look, Botox, or a need to look younger or sexier, even though all these aspects of physical appearance have very little or nothing to do with obtaining happiness, and fulfillment.

Today, kids spend far too much time playing video games where the most common aim is to kill or destroy. While adults live a life of addiction, spending on things they don't need such as alcohol, cigarettes, gambling, sex, chocolate, gadgets… to name a few. Are these behaviours worthwhile – exhibiting values that create character or personality?

> **Most people are part of The SUPER-Generation™ which stands for Superficial Unfulfilled Pessimistic Egocentric & Restless #CorporateEscape**

I have coined the term **The *SUPER*– Generation™** (pronounced 'the super negative generation') to describe a group of people or a generation who focus their entire existence on anything external, so long as it moves and shines.

These people are **Superficial** because they mostly care about external things, like having a perfect body but without caring about their health, or spending money on the latest mobile phone when they can't afford their mortgage or rent. What is important has become reversed inside out. They care more about showing off, rather than feeling good about themselves. They want to be sure they possess the latest things and items so others can see how much they have as they attempt to project a feeling of importance through their possessions. Simplicity and relevance are completely alien concepts to them.

They are also **Unfulfilled** because their focus of attention is on external pleasures and quick gratifications, always wanting more without noticing how much they already have. For them there is always a feeling of 'never enough'. It's like trying to catch a butterfly that never stops moving. Their focus is on collecting things instead of living everyday experiences with the people they love. They are unable to recognise that the ordinary things are the ones that become extraordinary.

They are **Pessimistic** because they play the victim. It's always the system or others who are responsible for their situation. They are never happy with their lives and live from a place of scarcity, where others are seen as enemies, competitors or threats. Their glass is always half empty and they experience a feeling of resentment.

They are **Egocentric** because they think that the world turns around them just to fulfill their needs and wants, failing to notice that there are other people on the planet with their needs and wants too. They specialise in taking from others instead of sharing or giving. Their sense of balance and generosity doesn't have a 'world view'.

They are **Restless** because they are always trying to fit in more things, another call, another email, anything rather than being still and present. There is a feeling of 'not losing out', and 'not being left behind'. It's as if they were running an endless and exhausting race where there is no finishing line.

Can you recognise any of these patterns in your own behaviour, or in anyone you know? Even if you can, the good news though is that when you decide which values you want to live by and honour them in your daily life, then you can flip the coin to become part of **The SUPER+ Generation™**.

> ## *The New Entrepreneurs are The SUPER+ Generation™: Successful Unconventional Passionate Entrepreneurial & Relational #CorporateEscape* 🐦

The *SUPER+* **Generation™** (pronounced 'the super plus generation') are a group of people or a generation who are **Successful** because they don't wait for things to happen by magic or for others to make things happen for them. These professionals take responsibility for their own success and are willing to do what it takes to make it happen, but always in accordance with their values and their own definition of success. These are qualities that represent the New Entrepreneurs.

They are **Unconventional** because they rely on their own thinking. They use their mind to notice and relate to the world around them. They don't clutter their brain with irrelevant things and rubbish but nurture their mind and soul and are free thinkers.

They are **Passionate** because they care about others and the world around, wanting to make a difference to themselves and others. They do what they love and they are very good at it. Their passion is contagious and it comes across in everything they do. They are energetic and vital and people around them call them lucky and happy.

They are **Entrepreneurial** because they are willing to start again and again until what they want is achieved. They don't give up. They don't accept excuses and they find new ways to make things happen. They know they are Eagles and they soar with the wind until they find their right direction.

They are **Relational** because they care about people and they understand that what they do has an impact upon others. For them it's not about 'you' or 'me', it's about 'us' and how to make a 'win-win' situation for all.

Can you recognise aspects of yourself here? Yes? Then you are in a great position!

Action Step

1. Get two different coloured pencils – red and green – it doesn't matter, as long as they are sufficiently different.

2. Go back to **The *SUPER-* Generation™** list of qualities – Superficial, Unfulfilled, Pessimistic, Egocentric, Restless – and choose one colour and circle those that apply to you, and another colour for the ones that don't.

3. Do the same with **The *SUPER+* Generation™** list – Successful, Unconventional, Passionate, Entrepreneurial, Relational – but swap the colours round the other way.

4. Notice the proportions of each colour. Which colour have you used more of?

What do you notice here?

What is coming into your mind?

What can you do with these insights?

Your Notes

....

....

....

....

....

What Legacy Do You Want To Leave Behind?

When you come to understand that everything you say and do has an impact on yourself and on others, that everything is systemic, the vision you have for your life and the time you have here will expand as you grow.

You will start to become more concerned about other people and things beyond your own existence. You will begin to ask yourself deep meaningful questions and answer them with growing courage to transform the direction of your life. Let's find out more...

The Story Of The Emperor And The Horseman

A long time ago, there was an Emperor who told a man that he would give him the area of land that he could ride across. The man quickly jumped onto his horse and rode as fast as possible to cover as much land as he could. He rode and rode whipping the horse to go as fast as possible. And when he was hungry or tired, he did not stop because he wanted to cover as much land as possible. Finally, exhausted and near death he fell from his horse and onto the ground. As he lay there, he asked himself: 'Why did I push myself so hard to cover so much land when all I now need is a small piece of land in which to be buried?'

And the moral of this story?

The story is similar to the journey of your life. You push very hard every day to make more money and to gain power and recognition but, if you neglect your health, time with your family, and fail to appreciate the beauty that surrounds you, or the hobbies you love, then you have nothing. One day when you look back, you will realise that you don't really need that much, but then you won't be able to turn back time to recover what you have missed.

'People in the process of earning a living should not forget to live.'

Your Notes

....

....

....

....

....

You see people around you doing amazing things for others, and often you wish you could be like them. Well, have you ever thought that you have this desire because you already have the gift of being able to do things like this, inside you? You just need to learn to listen to your inner voice, to have the courage to take this thought outside your head and create a plan in the physical world to make it happen.

> *Greatness is contagious. Have the courage to bring your dream alive and others will help build your vision for a better world #CorporateEscape*

If you don't believe me, think of the Katrina Hurricane. Do you remember how the whole world offered support, money and all kinds of resources?

As humans, we feel compelled to help others because after all we are all social beings.

Whatever your goals are, moving from being an employee to becoming a New Entrepreneur requires a shift in mindset, and to better equip you to do that, there are four things you need to know about how your own brain works:

So, let's look at **The 4 Emotional Mirrors Of The Brain™** which are:

The First, the human brain cannot distinguish between emotional pain and physical pain, which is why we feel more connected to people when they are suffering rather than when things are all well. Remember the mirror neuron effect?

Second, you can't feel empathy for yourself only for others, which is why it is so important to be able to see things from others' perspectives. But, by becoming your own observer you can empathise with yourself and your circumstances, which in turn will enable you to support yourself better.

Third, research shows that people feel greater empathy when something bad happens to others rather than when people are happy, successful and all is well. Interesting isn't it? But never forget that your mind can be retrained and rewired.

Fourth, excitement and fear produce the same physical reactions in the body: palpitations, a faster heartbeat and sweaty palms. High performers know this well, so they teach their brain to equate one with the other by challenging themselves to do scary things, often extreme sports that make them feel scared and excited simultaneously. This is about training your brain for success!

After all, we are emotional beings wanting to make an impact on the world. You just need to decide what mark you want to make and then allow and encourage others to join you so that you create a community with shared values and a common vision!

Who Are You Born To Become?

Because society makes every possible effort to keep us under control throughout our lives, by telling us exactly what to do and how to perform, most of us fail to reach our full potential.

But, if you know:

- What your calling is
- Who you are called to become
- And what gifts you possess

Then you are able to break from society's control and will be able to create the life that you want and deserve.

> **The day you discover why you were born, what is your life mission and your life purpose, nothing and nobody can stop you from doing and becoming this person. No social norm, convention or prehistoric limiting belief will stop you, no gate-keeper, no obstacle will make you give up**

I once heard a quote that went something like: 'The two most important days of your life are, the day you were born and the day you discovered what you were born for.'

In order to get a deeper understanding of how your mind works, I would like you to think of your mind as being run by **Seven CEOs**, a useful analogy in a business context.

So, **The 7 CEOs Who Run Your Mind™** are:

The **First CEO is your conscious mind** that from before you were five has been running most of your life, a control freak when allowed to be, that gives orders and is the voice you hear inside your head.

The **Second CEO is your unconscious mind.** This one acts as a filing cabinet where each file has your emotions attached. The same thought can have different emotions though. This CEO only follows orders. Do you remember the **10 Rules To Empower Your Unconscious Mind™**, from Chapter 3? If you need to, take another look. By now you know that as humans we have a tendency to talk more about our negative emotions than our positive ones, an aspect I mentioned in the third of **The 4 Emotional Mirrors Of The Brain™**. So, you will need to create a habit to reverse this process by focusing more on your positive thoughts and emotions! I think that by now you start seeing the picture of why you do the things you do.

The **Third CEO is your heart,** and this has an intelligence all of its own. Your heart is the key to accessing information that includes and transcends what comes from your five senses. This CEO adds a new dimension to your intelligence, expanding your consciousness and empowering your mind, though your mind can only access this information via your heart.

It's important that you learn how to communicate with your multiple brains. Your heart knows when something isn't right and will tell you through your feelings, hunches and messages.

When your mind forces you to do something to which your heart says 'no', it will be hard work to make it happen because your will is a captive of your heart and not your mind. So, once you've chosen what you want to do, you will intellectually justify your choice and you will do it. On the other hand, when you do something that is congruent with both, it will happen effortlessly.

Some people lose their mind and get caught up in their heart. Others forget about their heart and become wrapped up in their mind. Neither way is good. The ideal is for both to talk to each other, something that can be done through imagery, using simple language and touch.

Your heart emits an electromagnetic field that surrounds your entire body and extending several metres in every direction beyond it. This electromagnetic field interacts with and is affected by anything that also has electromagnetic qualities, including the Earth itself, other people, plants, animals, space, the planets and even the stars. This field connects all of us to each other.

It also sends signals to every cell in your body, so affects your physical, mental, and emotional health and wellbeing. It's a powerful source of energy and information that literally tells all the cells in your body what to do.

The **Fourth CEO is your body,** which believe it or not tries to talk to you by using physical issues or illness to manifest something unexplored, emotional backlogs, blockages or situations that you've not taken care of. Seeing disease this way can help you to take control of your life not just by going to the doctor, but by also trying to figure out what needs to be looked at inside yourself, and dealt with once and for all.

By talking to your body and understanding the unresolved issues, you can begin to work at them so as to rejuvenate and renew yourself in ways you didn't think possible.

The **Fifth CEO is your intuition,** which the dictionary describes as either an ability to understand something immediately without the need for conscious reasoning; or a thing that one knows or considers likely from an instinctive feeling rather than through conscious reasoning.

Intuition is your ability to 'know' something without being able to explain it rationally or logically. It's that mysterious 'gut feeling' that allows you to quickly tap into your unconscious mind and access the 'archive' there that contains all kinds of information you don't remember at a conscious level.

Without intuition, you're no different from a computer, making decisions based on facts that often you don't even have. So, you're already making decisions based on various factors other than logic. Sometimes you pick up on things unconsciously without realising it, such as putting trust (or not) in somebody you've just met. This 'something' you have picked up will be registered as a certain 'feeling' that you can't articulate or explain at that precise moment but which often turns out to be right.

Your gut also has a functional and complex brain with memory and intelligence too, and like your heart, it too knows when something isn't right and will tell you through your feelings, premonitions and internal messages. You can communicate with this brain through simple language, imagery and touch. As you see, learning how to use your intuition can be very useful.

And it's called a 'gut feeling' for good reason because often when you make a decision that you 'know' is wrong, you'll feel discomfort in your stomach.

The **Sixth CEO is your life force energy.** This comes to you at birth and stays with you until your death. It's an energy that flows freely, like a hose connected to a water tap, but if there are knots in the hose, just as with water, it won't be able to pass through you.

If you don't feel in the 'flow', energised, awake or 'alive', then probably there is a knot or two in your hose that you need to untie. Often this blockage is created by doing things you don't want to do. So, if your job is not fulfilling, if you are doing it only for money and without love and passion, this is going to stop your life force energy from flowing, and you will feel unhappy and unfulfilled. So stop and remove the knots!

The mind is a like a machine that exists outside the constraints of time and space, but without spiritual guidance this machine operates on 'autopilot', empty, without life, meaning and joy.

The **Seventh CEO is your soul,** the reason why you are here, though this is often forgotten about. But when you discover your life purpose you will know what you're meant to do, and who the people are you want to do it with. There will then be a feeling of living your life to the full as though finally all the pieces of a puzzle have fallen into place. Life will feel good and every day will be good. There will be a feeling of joy, and you will feel blessed just to be alive! When you experience this you will know it for sure and that you have become connected with your soul. From this moment on, the meaning of your life transcends to a different level altogether.

Where Do You Want To Go?

It may seem like a simple question, but think hard (and frankly!) about it. If you're to live a fulfilling life then it's essential that you have a goal – a mission – that is powerful enough to supersede and replace any familiar paradigms and patterns of your existing thinking.

Speaking from personal experience, my mission has always been to empower people to believe in themselves so they have the courage to live their lives on their own terms, both personally and professionally.

Although I've moved through many different careers over the course of my life, this has always been the common thread that has united them and so I have never done anything that didn't allow people to feel better about themselves.

Nowadays, as part of my mission, I deliver workshops and coaching programmes that enable professionals like you to find:

CLARITY, about what is next for you in your life.

PURPOSE, so that you can find out what it is that you are born to do and create.

VISION, so as to develop a broader vision for your life, one that embraces all areas and creates a life/work balance that is right for you and your loved ones.

COURAGE, so that you might develop your emotional resilience by stretching your current mindset, beliefs, habits and paradigms and breaking free from your current constraints.

LEVERAGE, so as to find the best ways to use your experience, knowledge and skills to fulfill your life purpose and mission in a way that feels true to you and brings prosperity into your life.

IMPLEMENTATION, so as to create a step-by-step plan that will make your vision a reality and enable you to achieve success on your terms and in a way that is achievable and measurable.

When you are clear about your mission, the prospect of change suddenly becomes much less intimidating because there is an inner knowledge about what is right for you and what is not, enabling you to identify your next steps.

> *Don't be afraid to set goals that both excite and scare you! If you don't, then the odds are that you're still operating within your familiar patterns of thinking. Your main goal should be strong enough to imprint itself on your unconscious mind so that it is the driving force behind each and every decision you make*

If you want to stay in your old, out-of-date world, expecting continuous employment or successful self-employment by using old business models, then there is no need to do anything but just wait to be steamrollered by a fast-changing world.

LIFE IS ABOUT CHOICES

However, if you want to get ahead, then read on because the next section explains why people find change so difficult, what you can do about it, and how a catalyst can help you go where you want to go, safer and faster.

> **Key Ideas To Take Away**
> 1. Life is about making choices, but unless these are made on the basis of your values and convictions, then your life will feel pointless and unfulfilled. Whatever your goals, you need to understand about **The 4 Emotional Mirrors Of The Brain™** in order to shift your mindset from being an employee to becoming a New Entrepreneur successfully.
> 2. Regardless of your current working reality you need to look wider and deeper at your constraints and opportunities. Don't allow yourself to become complacent, you must always keep your skills up-to-date. You need to create a plan B.
> 3. There is more to life than money, and if it doesn't feel right for you, then you are going off track. Revisit who and what matters in your life, and change the proportions of each until you achieve a balance that's best for you. It's your life so don't give your power away.
> 4. Make a choice about whether you want to be part of **The *SUPER–* Generation™** (Superficial, Unfulfilled, Pessimistic, Egocentric and Restless) or **The *SUPER +* Generation™** (Successful, Unconventional, Passionate, Entrepreneurial and Relational). There is no in between.
> 5. **The 7 CEOs Who Run Your Mind™** are there to guide you to a meaningful life, but to do that, they all need to be nurtured if they are to remain alive!

Your Notes

In Chapter 5, you will learn…

Why change is difficult – which is why it is often viewed as a threat – and why you need to retrain your mind if you are to succeed in any change process. Your brain is wired to resist change and so you have to develop over time a natural preference to deal with any type of new or challenging situation. 'Moving away' is a fear-based preference and 'moving towards' is pleasure and reward-based. The good news is that you can retrain your mind at any time to achieve different results. We'll look at homeostasis and how it affects your behaviour and who you are, and understanding that will help you to stop trying quick one-week diets and quick fix solutions!

The main prison you find yourself locked in is your mind. Your routines, habits and paradigms keep you trapped in your old ways of being and doing and it's crucial that you update them, otherwise change will remain a painful process and becoming a successful New Entrepreneur will be elusive. To make this easier you need to have a strong motivator and the help of a change catalyst who can guide you through and ease the process to achieve success.

Part II

Purpose

"There is one quality which one must possess to win, and that is definiteness of purpose, the knowledge of what one wants, and a burning desire to possess it."

Napoleon Hill

Chapter 5

Change Is Difficult Until You Know Why And How

Everything you experience today is the cumulative result of every single decision you've ever made. It therefore follows that if you don't change your patterns of thinking, you'll keep making the same sort of decisions, and your life will remain the same.

The problem is that your life can't remain the same.

I meet plenty of people who know where they are and where they want to be, but never act on that knowledge due to a combination of fear, apathy and inertia. They're reluctant to follow (or even acknowledge) their dreams because they are scared to fail and confused about how to get started.

Does any of this sound familiar?

Let me share with you this story about the Chicken Eagle, which I like very much as it reminds me that you should chase your destiny and to be who you are meant to be. It also illustrates how you need to be careful not to conform, otherwise you will just become a reflection of the people you mix with.

The Chicken Eagle Story

At the edge of the woods, near a small farm, a baby orphaned eagle fell from its nest to the ground, where it lay, not yet able to fly. A farmer found the eagle, and thinking it was one of his own chickens, brought it to the coop so that it could be with the other chicks and mother hens.

As time passed, the baby eagle grew and it learned to do what chickens do, pecking grain from the ground and drinking from the watering trough. It kept its eyes on the ground and strutted around in circles, looking just like an over-sized chicken as it scratched the ground for grubs and worms, and even trying to make early morning wake-up calls.

Since chickens can't fly, the eagle never tried to spread his wings and leave the coop, because he didn't know that he could. Whatever the chickens did, the eagle did because he thought he was like them.

One day, a neighbour came to visit his friend the chicken farmer and was surprised to see the eagle strutting around the chicken coop, pecking at the ground, and acting like a chicken. When the farmer explained that he had brought the bird to the coop as a chick and only later discovered that it was an eagle, since the eagle had been raised as a hen, it actually believed it was one.

Then one day another eagle flew over the barnyard. The eagle in the coop looked up and wondered: 'What kind of creature is that? How graceful, powerful, and free it is.'

So, he asked another chicken what it was.

'That's the eagle, the king of the birds,' the chicken told him. 'He belongs to the sky and we belong to the earth. You will never be able to fly like that.'

One day the gate of the coop was left open and the eagle wandered out and about the farm, but scared of the unknown, he went quickly back to the other chickens with whom he thought he belonged. But during that night he remembered what it felt like to be out of the confined space, it was a mixture of fear and excitement that he wanted to experience once more.

So, a few weeks later, when the gate was left open again the eagle went out and this time explored further afield. He knew he would feel scared but he also knew how to get back to the coop if his fear became too much.

Seeing a mountain in the distance, he headed towards it, picking at grain and worms on his way.

As he did so, the eagle that had flown over the farm saw him and landed beside him and said: 'What are you doing here and why do you walk that way pecking at the ground?'

'Because I am a chicken,' said the young eagle, 'and this is what chickens do'.

'But you aren't a chicken,' said the other eagle, 'and you belong to the sky not to the ground!'

'My friend,' he went on, 'you were born an eagle with the heart and the spirit of an eagle, and nothing can change this. You were born to soar. If you don't want to accept your greatness, it is better that you die here today on the rocks below than live the rest of your life being a chicken, out of your own world and gawked at by others. So, follow me to the top of the mountain and I will show you that you are an eagle and that you can fly.'

The young eagle was scared but curious because he wanted more from his life.

'What if I'm an eagle after all,' he said to himself, remembering the magnificent bird he had seen flying high in the sky and dreaming of how he could fly like that one day.

When they reached the top of a high mountain, they could not see the farm nor the chicken coop. The older eagle lifted the younger one onto his outstretched wings and flew high into the sky where the bright sun was beckoning above.

He said: 'You are an eagle! You belong to the sky and not to the earth so stretch your wings and fly.'

The chicken eagle stared up into the awaiting sky, straightened his body and opened his wings and began to move them, slowly at first, until suddenly he was in the air, rising powerfully in ever-higher spirals as he rode the unseen thermals of hot air – until he was no more than a speck against the sun.

> **Exercise 16**
> 1. In what parts of your life are you 'playing small' right now? Think of examples in your own professional and personal life.
> 2. What would it be like for you to soar like an Eagle? Think of an area of your life where you could fly like one.

Your Notes

Why Are You So Afraid Of Change? And, Why Is Your Brain To Blame?

Your Brain Is Wired To Resist Change

You may have asked yourself why it is that every time you say to yourself that you are going to do something differently you still keep doing the same old things?

So, you know somebody who wants to quit smoking and has been trying for ages? They stop for two months, sometimes longer, and then something happens that triggers them to start again. The important thing to understand here is that few smokers smoke because they love it; for most of them, smoking is a substitute for something else, a strategy to deal with boredom, stress and shyness and much besides, though it's the *reason* why they do this that matters most.

As human beings, we're hardwired to resist change. So, your brain will always gravitate towards minimising risk while maximising reward. Do you remember the story of the Eagle at the beginning of the book? It needed to make a choice: to either move away from dying or to move towards change in order to survive and thrive for another thirty years.

CHANGE IS DIFFICULT UNTIL YOU KNOW WHY AND HOW

And in the chicken eagle story you've just read, the eagle needed to move away from the familiar, limiting existence of 'being' a chicken and move towards a new model, accepting his greatness, gifts and challenges so that he could soar and fly! And this is the same choice you'll need to make to become a New Entrepreneur.

Let's deal with these two main preferences – 'moving towards' and 'moving away from' – in more detail. Take a look at the diagram below.

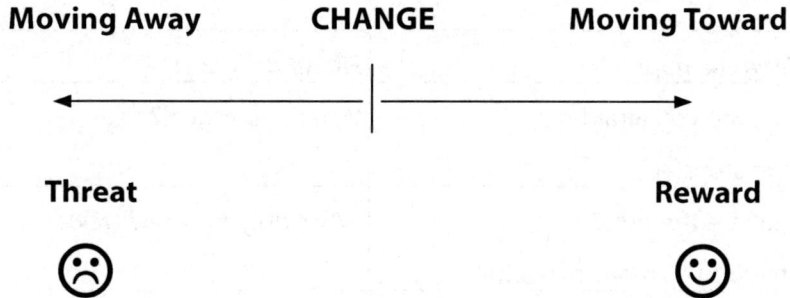

These are the characteristics that describe each of these two behaviours.

Characteristics of 'Away' vs Toward Behaviour	Characteristics of 'Toward' vs Away From Behaviour
Flight	Fight
Minimise danger and possible pain	Maximise reward and the possibility of pleasure
Approach: Critical of the situation, looking for the risk	Approach: seeking to reach goals and objectives
Focus: Emphasis on problems. Avoids problem finding and solving	Focus: Emphasis on solutions
Disengagement	Engagement
Uncertainty	Curiosity and interest
Tunnel vision. Narrow view	Peripheral vision. Global view
Hostility	Approachability
Look for security measures (crime)	Better world where we want to live

Characteristics of 'Away' vs Toward Behaviour	Characteristics of 'Toward' vs Away From Behaviour
Challenge of this preference:	*Challenge of this preference:*
Easy to miss opportunities	Insufficient evaluation and testing of ideas
Not knowing where to go	Not always learning from the past
Filling the gaps:	*Filling the gaps:*
What are you afraid of?	What's your goal?
What stops you?	
What are the risks?	What do you want? (reward)
What do you want to avoid?	
How could you make this work?	What else could you do?
What would be the way to do this?	What other ideas does this evoke?

As you can see, both preferences are quite different, and using one more than another will have a profound effect on your life. The more you are able to overcome your fears and accept change, the happier and more fulfilled you will become!

Here's some food for thought. The eminent psychologist Abraham Maslow believed that only 2% of people achieved self-actualisation (that is the fulfillment of one's full potential). Consequently, most people live unfulfilled lives defined by apathy, conformity and wasted potential. They are living like chickens without realising they have the heart, the strength and the potential of an Eagle.

Hopefully, the fear of living your life like a chicken is much more powerful than the fear of going after your dreams.

Your brain is very smart and is trained easily, though most think the opposite. This means that even when you are doing things you don't like, if you repeat them often enough, your brain figures that this must be something important to you, and so makes the effort to learn it. This is how bad habits become ingrained.

This means that you must be careful about what you do if you don't want to train your mind to do the opposite of what you ultimately want.

One of the most important functions of your brain is to ensure your safety.

This means that while it processes the masses of information it continually receives, it needs to quickly work out whether something is dangerous to you or not, so that it can alert you.

The mind doesn't like sudden changes, it likes repetition and routine. Once your mind creates a new pathway it is more than happy to stick with it; however these pathways need to be created in the first place. This can be achieved by stretching yourself doing different things that become habitual. Like the chicken eagle, once he realised he could fly he was able to do it any time at will, naturally and effortlessly.

What Is Homeostasis And What Has It To Do With You?

There is a psychological concept called homeostasis. This describes a process by which the mind tries to override any new behaviour that the body forces the mind to do.

Remember how your **7 CEOs Who Run Your Mind™** interact with one another? How your heart knows first before your mind? How your body holds information that is passed to your conscious and unconscious mind?

Homeostasis affects your behaviour and who you are by preventing your body from making drastic changes, to maintain stability in your life, even if to keep doing what you're doing is detrimental to you.

As an example, when an obese person starts exercising, homeostasis tries to make the body resist the activity in order to maintain stability. So, if suddenly you want to lose six pounds or three kilos a week, and attempt this only through eating the very minimum, you will not lose any weight because the mind will work out ways to compensate and keep you safe.

Alternatively, if you start going to the gym for ten hours a week having never gone before, your body's safety mechanism would be triggered to protect you from losing any weight too fast because this could put your whole system at risk.

It's not that the strategies themselves will not work, it's just that the mind will look for alternative ways to compensate for the changes, so that in the end, you do not lose weight because maintaining stability is your mind's primary concern. This is why it's far more effective to try to lose weight slowly, as this gives your mind and body time to adjust, so your mind will not rebel.

The same happens with sudden, working life events, turning points that blow your mind away. Your mind will look for safety first.

I remember the Friday afternoon when I was told to collect my things and not to come back to work on Monday as my job was no longer available. I knew this was not true, in fact my boss's wife had been bored at home and decided to take my job. She had already started coming to the office more and more, always choosing to sit by me to see what I was doing. Even though the reason for her sudden interest was clear, being made redundant overnight was not something I had expected.

At first, I was shocked and felt empty, then scared, tearful and then ashamed. What was I going to tell my parents, my boyfriend, my friends? I decided not to say anything to anybody apart from my boyfriend, as he was bound to find out.

I needed time to figure out what I was going to do for the rest of my life and to create a plan for moving forward first. I wanted to take my own decisions and I wasn't inclined to listen to everybody else's ideas and opinions about what I should do next. I was 28, and living in a foreign country, so 'What's next for me?' was all I kept asking myself. I didn't want to talk about it; I just wanted to find another job and move on with my life, or at least to have answers to my questions and be able to see a light in the fog.

Everlasting Change Requires A Strong Motivator. Do You Know Your WHY?

We have already looked at how certainty is an illusion, a fallacy and a false friend, and there was a part of me then that wanted the same security, to find another job and carry on as before. But there was also another part of me that wanted to do something more exciting, especially having started my working life as a freelance fashion designer in Paris.

Since the age of fourteen, I had always wanted to be my own boss, to have my own business, so, being employed never felt right for me. I had a mixture of emotions: fear on the one hand about not finding another job or being able to pay my rent; and on the other hand, the excitement of the possibility of at last starting my own business.

As you know, the brain sees anything new as a threat, but then I didn't know that the brain couldn't distinguish between fear and excitement and produce the same physical reaction to both. Back then I was not sure what I was feeling, but I felt scared and without any other choice than to work out a plan and do something about it, and the quicker the better.

From my story you will probably recognise the two natural preferences mentioned above for dealing with any situation: *'Moving away'* from the things you don't like, or *'Moving towards'* achieving something that do you want.

In my case I was 'moving away' from working for somebody else and 'moving towards' starting my own business. Both options were scary, but at least I was clear that I didn't want to leave my life and destiny in somebody else's hands again, and that's what I would be doing if I chose to work as an employee and I was made redundant again at 38, 47 or 53!

This option was scarier to me than starting my own business even though I didn't have a clue about what to do, or how to do it.

This shows that it's very important you have a strong motivator for change as this will keep you going through the tough times and self-doubting moments. It's crucial you know your *why*?

All humans are scared of change at one level or another. It's normal, and by now you know that every time you try to do something new, from learning a new language, to working abroad, to starting a family, to getting married, to buying and selling a house, from moving jobs, from starting a new relationship, to become a New Entrepreneur... you are sure to experience both fear and excitement.

Depending on your life experience, you will have developed a natural preference for 'moving away' or 'moving towards' things and situations, but this preference is contextual. In other words, you may have a natural 'move away' preference for certain areas of your life and a 'moving towards' preference for other areas.

Neither preference is better nor worse than the other, as each has strengths and challenges, so ideally you will be able to develop flexibility so you can choose the approach that's best suited for the task and issue at hand.

When you have a strong *why* for change then you become unstoppable. All pioneers are scared and at the same time excited about discovering new ways of doing things. However, they chose to face fear to make things better for others and themselves; true Leaders are scared to make the wrong decisions and fear the implications of doing so, yet they accept their mission to support and lead others by finding new ways where none is obvious; the visionaries will walk untraced roads long before others even think these roads may exist at all, because they care much more about the wellbeing of others than anything else.

Exercise 17
1. Look at the different areas of your life. Where do you need to make changes right now so that you can be who you want to be?
2. Why are these changes important?

Your Notes

N.B. There are more bonus exercises for this section in your Resources Pack, online. Go to: **www.maitebaron.com/resourcepack**

If you feel more often scared than excited, go deeper. Find your strong *why* – a major reason to change what you know needs to be changed in your life. Become an Eagle before it's too late. If you allow fear to control your life, then you will carry on being a follower and will always be scared, living a mediocre and uninspiring life, someone who is easily replaced and superseded.

You have your life in your hands, choose wisely. Make sure you have the right support in place; it takes time, training and discipline to know how to do this alone, but the effort is worth it. Never view asking for help as a weakness, rather it's a strength, after all by asking you are already taking action!

How You Train Your Brain Will Determine The Level Of Success You Can Achieve

Most people believe that their brain is as it is from birth, and that you are either intelligent or not, and that intelligence is a lottery. This is not true at all!

Scientists talk today about the 'plasticity' of the brain, its ability to reshape itself to grow and expand. You have already heard about some cases when after an accident or loss of a sense, the brain has 'reshaped' itself so as to compensate for the weakness.

And the truth is, you are retraining your brain every day, which means you can take conscious actions to make it expand or shrink.

Unfortunately, most brains become atrophied after their owners have finished university or college. I'm tired of listening to professionals, from their 30s to their 60s, who think they know it all and that there is nothing for them to learn any more. They believe that they have done well in their own way, and that there is no point looking at things from a different perspective. I know you are not one of them, otherwise by now you would not still be reading this book.

Again, this all starts in your childhood when you were rewarded for being a follower and discouraged from being an Eagle. Every time you stood out, behaved or acted in a different or nonconformist way, you were punished for being too creative or doing something different. Sooner or later, you learned the social consequences of being yourself. The trick now is how to balance both, to be you, and to be able to survive with social norms and conventions.

You have become very good at creating routines, habits, forming beliefs and living between the limits of your own paradigms. All this has helped you to get where you are now. But today, you are revisiting your life, looking at the many years you have ahead of you, and creating for you a second chance, an opportunity to reformat your life in the way you want, all the way forward. To understand that you can break free from the conformity mould and become a New Entrepreneur.

There is another dimension to all this, your paradigms. These are the social beliefs and values that have been passed to you from previous generations, from the culture you live in, from your own family context and so on. These are often invisible and yet in most cases they influence the most important decisions you make, without you really being aware of it. These are a clear example of the impact of society; indoctrination and socialisation in your own life, and which in effect mean you become not much more than a spectator.

The Impact Of Routines, Habits And The Homeostasis Process

We are creatures of our own automatic reactions and habits that started forming the day we were born and are still evolving today. Your responses to situations you face are programmed by your belief system, which has been shaped by the events in your life to date. But success can't happen if you stick with yesterday's habits, routines and experiences, trying to use them to determine tomorrow's actions. Unless you do something different you won't achieve different results!

The Buzzard, The Bat, and the Bumblebee

If you put a buzzard in a pen that's one metre square and open at the top, in spite of its ability to fly the bird will stay where it is. This is because a buzzard must have room to take off. Without the three or four metres it needs, it will not even attempt to fly, and so will remain a prisoner for life in a small jail with no top.

The ordinary bat that flies around at night is a remarkable and nimble creature in the air, yet it cannot take off from a level place. If it is placed on flat ground, all it can do is shuffle helplessly and, no doubt, painfully, until it reaches some slight elevation from where it can throw itself into the air. Then, at once, it takes off like a flash.

A bumblebee if dropped into an open tumbler will stay there until it dies, unless it is taken out. It never sees the means of escape at the top, but persists in trying to find some way out through the sides near the bottom. It seeks a way where none exists, until it destroys itself.

And the moral of this story?

Many people are like the buzzard, the bat and the bumblebee, struggling with all their problems and frustrations, not realising that the answer is right there above their head!

> **Exercise 18**
> 1. Which one of these behaviours sounds most familiar to you, the buzzard, the bat, or the bumblebee?
> 2. What analogies from your own life can you draw from this story?
> 3. What habits do you need to change to achieve different results?
> 4. What are you going to do about this? Hint: create a simple and specific plan with achievable and measurable results.

Your Notes

So, how do your routines and habits impact on your long-term achievements? To see that, you first need to understand the difference between routines and habits and a little more about how your mind works.

Routines are conscious thoughts you have self-programmed into your mind because of a need. For instance, this could be a need to earn money and so a need to keep your job, even if you hate it. Routines mean you consciously take the same action to get the same results. Every day you get up at the same time, go to work in the same way, do what you must do to get your pay cheque at the end of the month, always on the same day.

Habits on the other hand, are unconscious patterns of behaviour that allow you to react automatically to a known situation in the same way every time to get the same results, like brushing your teeth after eating, preparing your briefcase the night before or writing a 'to do' list for tomorrow.

Both routines and habits are important because they save a lot of your brain energy, so making it available for other more complex tasks. At the same time, these automatic responses bring some important challenges, because their 'auto-pilot' behaviour can take control of some of the most important decisions of your life, such as which job or which type of relationship you are looking for. You might think that this is not the case, but do you keep going for the same sort of jobs, and do you end up in similar kinds of relationships facing very similar types of challenges every time?

This brings us back to homeostasis as it's the main factor that will stop you from changing your habits because your brain sees anything other than slow change as dangerous.

As you can see, this presents a conflict between what society and the media wants you to do, and what your mind and body knows is best for you. You can see this particularly in today's working environment, which only encourages fast change and quick results.

Yet, from scientists around the world who are studying the neuroscience of the brain, there is enough evidence to suggest that forcing change is not the way to make change happen, even though this is what we are continually trying to do.

Given this, it's hardly surprising that 70% of organisational change initiatives fail.

I find this blindness surreal.

We are obsessed with numbers and statistics and yet at the same time we seem unable to interpret the results. We have a natural ability to delete, distort and generalise information so as to cope with it. However, this doesn't mean that the numbers don't speak for themselves!

The bottom line is that you can't change behaviour without shifting the mindset first. Organisations keep throwing away huge amounts of money in pointless quick-results leadership programmes that are a waste of time and energy, resulting in superficial changes that look good from the outside.

I call this 'cosmetic work' and it is like a decorator covering the cracks of a wall before putting the property on the market, but without tackling the real issues. All this does is increase people's resistance and disengagement and ultimately push them towards becoming a New Entrepreneur.

By acting this way, these toxic orgnisations shove their Eagles away, leaving behind only the Chickens who are too scared to leave and fly.

> *Organisations are shooting themselves in the foot and then complaining about talent shortage. There is not a shortage of talent, there is however a shortage of leaders able to recognise, develop and foster talent*

This is the main reason why I've shifted my attention to wanting to develop entrepreneurial Eagles outside organisations instead of wasting my time trying to make a difference inside organisations, where all the focus is on ensuring that remaining employees continue to behave like Chickens. While the internal politics, the gatekeepers and the egos at the top keep running the show, trying to develop new Leaders in the corporate world is a dream that will never happen.

There is a global leadership crisis at every level of organisational and political structure as well as society as a whole. The only real solution is for people to take responsibility for their lives, by becoming Self-Leaders, seeking self-development and self-actualisation so they can reach a greater level of consciousness about what matters and what is going on. Then Eagles can stop being corporate Chickens and be free to become New Entrepreneurs.

There are plenty of 'little leaders', the Chickens who are in positions of power, with a title and a big office, lots of plumage, but without the courage, the integrity and the values necessary to create social change for the best.

That's why most leaders delegate most leadership development to others, often the HR department. I'm sorry, but a Leader needs to be involved heart and soul with this task, which is probably one of the most important ones after all, because it will be one of their main legacies. Profit is important yes, but at the same time no more so than developing leaders.

When you leave, profits will go up or down, you have no control over the future, even though you may love to believe otherwise, but if you have developed Eagles then they will be able to find their way forward.

Without this, an organisation becomes a mere commodity in danger of extinction. Without heart and soul leadership doesn't exist. Leadership and leader are words well used today, but as with many others, they have very little meaning.

> *In a world of language inflation Leadership and Life/Work Balance are words that contain letters but no meaning #CorporateEscape*

The Importance Of The Emotions On Your Decision-Making Process

You need to wake up and start noticing:

- Who is taking the decisions for you?
- Which factors are impacting your decisions?
- Where do these factors come from?
- And more importantly, who is responsible for them?

Why do you keep going through the motions, acting like a brainless Chicken, without using the beautiful mind you are given to soar and thrive like an Eagle?

Yes, you may be hurt, people will disagree with you, and you may lose some friends because they don't understand what you are doing and so on. But, this is not so bad. Friends that only like you when you are like them are not friends at all, just acquaintances. Real friends will support you even when they disagree with you, as they will understand and respect what is important for you. Real friends want you to grow, to be happy, to move on with your life.

So, be more selective about your friends because 'not all that shines is gold', after all.

Some people become uncomfortable when you move on with your life, because they feel scared to be left behind. If you move forward what will happen with them? Do you remember the need for safety? Well this will keep kicking in all the time!

When people see you succeed, they will either feel inspired to do something different for themselves or will feel resentful, jealous and critical of you. Unfortunately, the second option is easier and more popular than the first.

> **There will always be Eagles and Chickens but this is not decided at birth, nor by colour, nor religion, nor the family into which you were born. Being a Self-Leader is not an accident, it's a conscious decision made by ordinary people who are willing to become New Entrepreneurs to do unconventional things and to live extraordinary lives**

Like this they can keep going along without making any effort to change anything themselves, apart from complaining about why you are so lucky and they are not.

If you are stuck in your old ways of being and doing then you haven't developed the muscles you need for change. If you feel uncomfortable with foreigners or people who have different views to yours; if you feel threatened by people who hold different beliefs, or are from a different race, or have a different religion, then you haven't developed a taste for change and you will just keep repeating your same old story. This is not what living is about and you will be wasting a golden opportunity to grow and self-develop without giving it a second thought.

Why Resisting Change Is Sucking Your Life Away And Damaging Your Health?

The Main Reason Why Most People Resist Change Is Through Fear, Purely And Simply

The more you resist change the more vulnerable you become, emotionally and physically. By now you know that any new experience you go through you will experience as a threat. Do you remember the power of your unconscious mind? Most people view change as something to resist, even if it's for the best. Doing nothing is always perceived as safest.

When I talk to professionals like yourself about their desire to escape corporate, or to make a radical change in their lives to become a New Entrepreneur, fear is often and for most the main reason for their resistance and inertia, keeping them unhappy and stuck.

Fear is not going to disappear on its own so you need to learn how to deal with it effectively. After all, there will always be reasons and new situations to feel fearful about. This is why it's so important you get the right support and learn how to deal with it so you can make it an ally and move courageously forward in your life.

You need to learn how to rewire your brain, and then when you know how to do it you will realise that it's possible to be in full control of your mind, while also being emotional and feeling alive at the same time.

In order to do this, you need to start with small steps. Remember the homeostasis principle that will make sure that your system stays in safety?

So, begin by taking small challenges, talking to strangers, resist that craving for a chocolate, take a class in a subject that interests you but you don't know much about. Small and ongoing steps will take you far.

You need to be willing to be uncomfortable for a while to learn and stretch your mind through willpower and discipline if you are to develop further.

Learning to delay gratification will allow you to stop giving up at the first sign of difficulty, and help you stay motivated throughout the process by knowing that where there is a will there is a way.

This is not a one off, but a continuum as your mind gets used to overcoming challenges. And, the better you become at it, the easier it is to tackle new challenges, so it feels right from the beginning.

Embrace Your Fear!

You often look at fear as something to be avoided, but if you never experience fear or excitement then you're almost certainly not learning anything. A reluctance to push through your fear means that you will remain bound by familiar habits, routines and paradigms forever. So, have the courage to make small changes to your daily behaviour and it will not be long before you start seeing dramatic improvements in your life.

Fear is like a little monster that you can handle to start with, but if you keep feeding it then it will become so big that it will get out of control, heavy and oppressive. Then it will eat you from the inside, until a time will come when your fear is so big that you can't hide it inside any longer and then everyone will notice it too.

Fear starts with the little things that you don't do or should do. You stop calling clients because you are fearful of rejection; you stop sending CVs because nobody will be interested. You stop taking risks in your job so you can't make mistakes. You stop expressing your views in a relationship in case they are 'wrong'. You start losing your self-confidence and this affects your self-esteem. Eventually your lack of willpower impacts on every area of your life.

The 'Boiling Frog' Story

You may know the story (this is not an actual experiment by the way) of the frog which when dropped in a pan of boiling water immediately jumps out, but when put into a pan of cold water that's gradually heated to boiling, stays there until it boils to death. This is because the frog's survival instincts are geared towards detecting sudden changes not gradual ones.

And the moral of this story?

People get themselves into trouble by not noticing slow changes to their environment until it's too late. This story warns us to keep paying attention, not just to obvious threats, but also to more slowly developing ones. It illustrates the idea that change needs to be gradual to be accepted.

Let me give you an everyday example of this.

People read about rising unemployment figures in newspapers, and how the fast pace of change in the working environment is having an adverse effect on millions all over the world. Yet, most professionals do not create a plan B that may protect them from what might happen. Instead, they read the news as passive observers of their own reality, as if life has nothing to do with them until something occurs and they become the news. Like the frog in the gradually heating pan, they are unable to react and then complain about what is happening, feeling resentful and hopeless.

One of the side-effects of fear is that when you are in a fearful state your thoughts become blurred and you can't think straight. Things feel more difficult, and obstacles feel bigger than they really are. Caught by fear, you start spiraling down until like the bumblebee you can't seem to find the way out. You start feeling uneasy with people, you stop trusting your own judgment and in turn you distrust other people's too. You feel embarrassed to talk about it and so become more and more isolated. When fear starts growing like this, you need help to be able to observe what is happening and to understand that reality and your thoughts are two different things. You need to temporarily become an observer of what is happening so you can gain a different perspective and start seeing things the way they really are.

> **Exercise 19**
> Can you think of other examples when you behave like the boiling frog?

Your Notes

....

....

....

....

....

Wake up and take action, and start creating a plan B before you need it!

Fear Drains Your Energy And Steals Your Life Away

Living in a state of fear is highly debilitating and can have a physical impact upon your immune system and your sense of identity. Your level of energy falls, so you feel tired most of the time until even the little things feel a big effort, and you stop doing the things you used to enjoy like going to yoga on Wednesdays or meeting your friends after work for a meal on Friday. You feel like you're running in a hamster wheel, but don't know how to change your situation.

You are scared that if you get out of the wheel you will not be able to get back in. That if you take a break, when you come back you will have lost all your clients or someone else will be doing your job, that your skills will not be in demand, and so on.

You are continually near to tears and so stressed that you feel vulnerable to everyday situations. You feel overly sensitive and everything seems to have an impact on you in a big way, and yet at the same time, you find it difficult to feel, your physical senses seem numb.

Fear has overtaken everything.

There's despair in your soul, you can't find a way out and you know you can't carry on like this. Even doing mundane things feels painful.

Remember **The 7 CEOs Who Run Your Mind**™ and how their interaction affects everything you do? How your heart and mind are connected, and that your heart emits an electromagnetic field that surrounds your entire body extending beyond it by several meters in every direction? So, whatever you can feel, others can perceive.

You want to give up all together because you can't cope any longer, but you can't, because you need to pay your bills, finish the last job for which you have a tight deadline... you are probably already burned out, but don't know it.

You sense you are on the edge of something, even though you don't know what it is. There is a feeling that something will happen that will make you stop. You want to disappear to a desert island but you can't.

Many career men and women tend to try and keep all this to themselves; they don't want to talk to friends or colleagues about their emotions, fears and concerns because they think that this in some way is a sign of weakness, and that they should be strong enough to deal with these situations by themselves. Sometimes they think they can find temporary relief in a quick drink after work, but as time passes and the situation gets worse the quick drink turns into evening long sessions, and then alcohol and food binges or drug abuse start to become a problem.

I had a client, around 38 at the time, a successful career woman working for one of the big corporations. She was continually stressed and at the end of her working day would work out at the gym before going home, then eating quickly, and then crashing into bed.

She had no other life outside her job and she filled her weekends with more work so as not to admit to the loneliness that was real in her life. Then one day she couldn't get up, she called in sick. She started to cry and couldn't stop.

She went to her doctor and was told she was burnt out and shouldn't go back to work until she was better able to cope. She was given antidepressants and referred to a psychologist. She was out of work for two years before a friend recommended coming to see me.

Understandably, the woman was very fearful about going back to work and was still crying for no apparent reason. Life felt intolerable and time was running out before she had to choose between going back to the same position or accepting voluntary redundancy. She felt that if she didn't go back, all her efforts to date would have been wasted and for nothing; she was also concerned about what her mother and friends would say about her being unemployed and with no idea about what she wanted to do next with her life.

Together we started exploring what was going on with her beneath the surface, and began to talk about her wildest dreams and her deepest fears, and what would she be doing in her ideal life?

This brought to the fore that in her dream life she would have her own business, though was not sure what. So, we began looking at her hobbies, things she was good at and the things she enjoyed doing. As we did this it also became clear that she wanted a family but didn't have a stable relationship. Deep down she was scared that if she had carried on working as she was, she would never have time to meet her Mr Right with whom to have a family. Can you see how things were unfolding?

Her body was crying out with exhaustion, stress, lack of self-care; her spirit was suffering because she felt trapped in a system and couldn't find a way out; and her emotional self was feeling more and more isolated and unable to cope. Her breakdown allowed her to regain control of her life.

The moral of this true story is that you don't need to wait for this to happen to you, you can choose what you want to do with your life right now. You don't need to damage your health to stop, when you already know that something needs to change.

So, ask for help as soon as you realise that something is not right. This is not a sign of failure or weakness, but a sign of intelligence that shows you understand that there is a need for another perspective and to gain a breathing space where you can look at your life anew. This is where somebody outside your normal circle can bring a new objectivity, especially if this is combined with the right skills that are needed to support you the way you need.

I like to think of periods of change as travelling. Sometimes you decide you need a trip for yourself, while at other times it's forced upon you. You may meet fellow travelers along your way who won't necessarily be travelling on the same route, or for the same distance, or towards the same destination.

It's this element of uncertainty that causes you to fear change; you want to feel like you're in complete control of your life at all times so anything that challenges this comfortable illusion is perceived as a threat. But it is unrealistic to expect to know in advance what is going to occur at each stage of your journey – all you can do is prepare yourself as best you can and accept what comes gracefully.

As soon as you start thinking about making changes in your life, you take the first step on a new journey. There are many things to think about at this stage, such as where do you want to go? How long will it take to get there? Will it be a pleasant experience? How are you going to make it happen?

All these questions can appear overwhelming, prompting you to retreat to your comfort zone and your old habits, routines and paradigms. There's no doubt that change requires openness, confidence and curiosity, but there's a way to accelerate your progress, and that's through a personal development catalyst.

In scientific terms, a catalyst is something that enables a reaction to occur more efficiently and it's the same with personal development. A catalyst is someone who can guide you through periods of change by increasing your emotional and intellectual perception and resilience in a way that will help make change faster and easier for you, so you can liberate energy sooner and apply it to other areas of your life.

A catalyst in the form of a personal development coach is easily one of the most effective ways to minimise your levels of pain and stress during periods of dramatic change in your personal or professional life and maximise the results you get. Just look at the following graph and you'll see what I mean.

CHANGE IS DIFFICULT UNTIL YOU KNOW WHY AND HOW

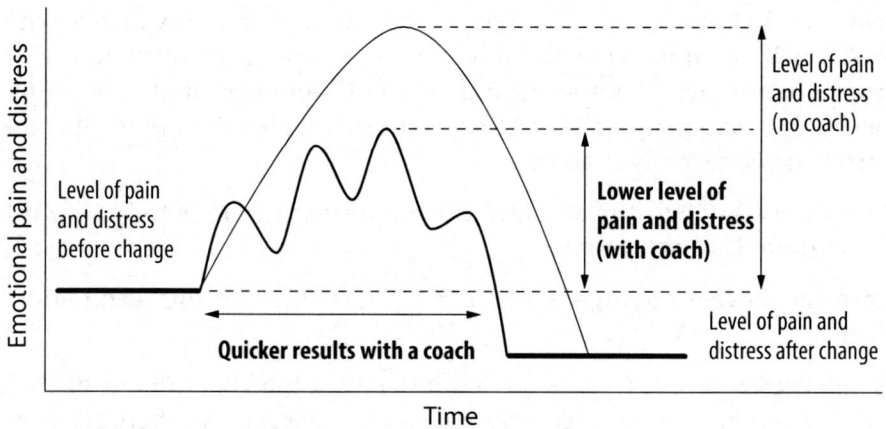

I love being a change catalyst, helping professionals like you dramatically reduce their levels of pain and distress during periods of significant change, such as escaping the corporate walls, going from employment to self-employment, starting your own business, dealing with redundancy or becoming a New Entrepreneur.

Life is always a compromise between risk and safety, between fear and excitement, between winning and losing, so finding a point of balance is the goal, but without involving a change catalyst this can become an impossible task for many, leaving them frustrated and disillusioned.

My clients know that when we work together there will be no more 'head-in-the-sand' moments – because they will be held accountable and kept focused on their long-term goals. This means that not only do they survive… but also thrive! There are moments in life when what you need is a quantum leap and I can give it to you.

Why Is It Important To Make Change Your Best Friend?
Because Otherwise Life Events Will Leave You Behind

Change is part of life. But just as with our boiling frog, it's easy to fail to see minor changes occurring around you. So, it's only when you meet friends you haven't seen for a long time that you notice how they have changed and then know that to them you must have changed too.

Without making change your best friend and learning how to deal with it you will be unprepared and ill-equipped to respond quickly to events and circumstances. Look at the financial crisis and the number of people who were caught up in it. It affects all of us, but some are feeling the effects more severely than others.

Some have savings; the amount is less important than getting into the habit of saving each month.

Some are always buying the latest gadgets, even when they can't afford them.

Some expect others to give them a job, either the government or their employer, while others create their own jobs especially as there are more and more opportunities to do this, and so anyone with a computer and an idea can be a potential New Entrepreneur.

Do you remember the table that described the characteristics of a 'dependent' employee and what is required to shift your mindset to become an 'independent' New Entrepreneur? (If you need to have another look, it's in Chapter 1.)

Let's face it; there are not enough jobs for the number of people who are out of work. This means that there are no longer careers or jobs for life, and unless you learn how to deal with what is happening in 'real time' and develop your mind in a way that can support you, you will sooner or later become unemployable and without a job.

On the other hand, when you start to update your beliefs and stop thinking that others will find solutions for you; when you start embracing the idea that you alone are responsible for keeping your skills up-to-date and finding solutions for yourself; this is when you will become self-reliant.

Now, it's time to create your plan B.

> **The future belongs to the New Entrepreneurs who can turn problems into opportunities to create new possibilities #CorporateEscape**

I remember coaching the CEO of a large company. He was complaining that employees who were hired seven or eight years ago were underperforming compared with the employees they were hiring now. I asked him if the skill set they were looking for seven years ago was the same as today?

'Of course not,' he said, and there was the problem.

The established employees hadn't kept their skill set up-to-date by adapting to the technological changes and market needs, while the organisation had also failed to create the right training to close the gap. Now these old employees would have to learn new skills fast or else be left behind, superseded by a more qualified and up-to-date workforce. This could have been avoided if both parties had taken their share of responsibility.

There Is Nothing Attractive In Being Dependent

The point I want to make here is that even if you are still employed today, *you* still need to be leading your own career because nobody else is going to do it for you. You need to have the courage to be ready to become independent at any time, otherwise you will always be dependent on others, reliant on them making things happen for you, or not, as will probably will be the case.

Sadly you will end up feeling stuck and trapped once more.

Exercise 20

Look at your life in the present as a temporary situation, and try to imagine a larger vision for yourself and your life ahead.

1. How can you use your free time differently to help you progress?

2. What area or areas of your life require attention?

3. What skills do you know you need to learn or improve?

Your Notes

Be active with a purpose, don't just do things to fill up your time. Reframe the way you look at time and the hours you have available to you. Your life is precious don't waste it, because there is no way back!

When Is The Best Time To Get Into Action?

As Soon As You Realise That Something Needs To Be Different

Nothing will change unless you take purposeful action and the perfect moment to do that is now. So, when you feel yourself trapped in a routine, doing things you have being doing for years that no longer feel right, or, when the purpose that you had is gone or no longer aligns with your current values, it's time to ask: Why am I doing this? and then to do something different.

Allow the answers to come to you, without judging them, then write them down and just notice what comes along.

If any area of your life feels like a 'black and white experience', this is a sure sign that change is required. Be open to explore what this might be, by looking for options and opportunities, opening your lens, and looking around and ahead.

If you stop bothering and caring about things that used to matter to you, because you can't find the time, because you are tired, because everything else seems to come first, it's time to reflect on what is really happening underneath. Probably the answer is: a fear of change, a fear of stopping or starting doing something, or a fear of taking a risk.

You Need To Take Action When You Know You Are Compromising Your Values

When you know that the only reason you keep doing what you are doing is to pay your bills, so that what you are doing doesn't matter or make any difference any more, then you feel like a fraud, living a stranger's life or a lie, and these are definitive signs of the need for a radical change. The moment you stop being you, nothing around you makes sense, so at this point you need to go back to the basics: Who am I? What do I want for my life?

Every day you are free to chose and restart the process until you get it right. It's not a matter or right or wrong but learning from each experience so that you know more about why you are here on this planet and how to bring your gifts alive to share them with others.

When You Feel That You Are Just Going Through The Motions

Your body is giving you signs that your mind keeps missing or dismissing. The feeling that you don't want to get up in the morning, or are tempted to stay in bed because you feel unwell, or that you are just living for the weekend? This is you going through the motions.

There is no middle point, either you feel alive or you are just surviving. The difference between these existences is enormous. When you feel alive, every day feels different, there is curiosity and a zest and you want to conquer the day and make the most of it. You know you need to put in some effort, but that is worth it, there is no pain, just lots of gain.

Instead of having one or two friends you hang around with, you enjoy meeting new people from different walks of life. Be interested in others and they will be interested in you.

You have many friends, some are like you and others very different. You understand that you can learn from anybody because you see people for who they are.

You need to create your life, your own reality, so if there is something you are not happy about, stop complaining and deal with it.

If you don't care about your own life, why should others? You may keep giving out the message that you are not important, but you are the one who matters most, and when you treat yourself with respect, you will matter to others and they will treat you with respect too.

> **Key Ideas To Take Away**
>
> 1. Change is difficult and requires willpower and training to undo all the baggage that you carry with you, which in turn affects every decision you take.
>
> 2. Your brain is wired to resist change, and you have a natural change preference which is to either 'move away' (fear-based) or 'move towards' (reward-based) a given situation. This matters because it will have an impact in every area of your life. The good news is that you can retrain your mind to achieve different results because as these preferences are contextual, you can easily learn how to map them across different situations.
>
> 3. Homeostasis affects your behaviour and who you are. Understanding that 'safety' for you is your mind's main concern will help you understand why it will override any decision the body takes. Change is a process and requires time. Don't sabotage your chances of success, instead be curious about change and how you can thrive and fly in any given situation.
>
> 4. Your existing routines, habits and paradigms keep you trapped in your old ways of being and doing. People around you don't want you to change and move on with your life because change is viewed as a threat for you and for them.
>
> 5. Change will remain a painful and unsuccessful process unless you have a strong motivator. A change catalyst can make all the difference, guiding you through and easing the process.
>
> 6. You need to look at fear differently. Remember that is by far the main reason that keeps you stuck and pushing away your dreams of becoming the New Entrepreneur you want to be, in charge of your own life.

Your Notes

....

....

....

....

....

....

In Chapter 6, you will learn…

That fear is a friend in disguise when you know how to keep it away. That fear is normal and it appears in exciting as well as stressful situations, visiting us all. You will find out how to enlarge your comfort zone to grow and evolve. You will realise how you already have all you need to take the next step in your life, whatever you choose this to be.

You will learn more about your change preferences, your values and your beliefs and how these become your drive, your strength and your motivation. Why you need to learn to be present, in the 'here' and 'now', if you want to live a quality life. You will also learn four simple strategies to keep your mind in the present, as this is the only place where you can make quality decisions that affect every area of your life.

Chapter 6

There Is Nothing To Be Afraid Of, Take Off And Learn To Fly

Fear Is A Friend In Disguise

By now you know that when you are in a process of change, fear is natural, and it visits everybody. What makes the difference is your ability to retrain your mind to flow with it. Fear appears in both threatening as well as exciting times, so it comes when you're looking for new clients or more work, when something unexpected happens to someone you know, when you feel that you're being left behind, or stuck in the past, when you doubt your future and ask yourself: What if the best of my professional life is already gone?

Every time I've changed career, even when I was transitioning my skills, it felt like crossing into a new territory where I was alone. It was as though I had to build the whole house again with new foundations, designs, and furniture. All had to be created from scratch. It's scary to start from zero, attracting new customers, promoting yourself, and getting things rolling!

When a relationship comes to an end, you fear you'll never find someone else, and that you will end up living alone for the rest of your days, imagining seeing all your friends having families and moving along with their lives, while you remain stuck in the past. To have holidays on your own, being ashamed to go out for dinner alone... the list goes on.

After ten years being in a relationship, married and divorced within a year, I was, at 39, no longer a young woman by social standards, but still desirable. I remember thinking: I have no clue how the dating scene works nowadays.

I wanted to meet someone interesting in my everyday life, but that was not so easy because if I discounted all my clients, and all the friends of friends who were single, there was no one left.

Friends had told me about their experiences with internet dating, so I tried it with an open mind and explored what it might offer, because I knew that in order to achieve my goal I needed to stretch my comfort zone.

Once I was having a coffee in Starbucks by Goodge Street station, and ended up talking to an English woman who had married an American after just three months of meeting him online! She looked pretty happy as we chatted about our lives over a coffee.

I only ended up talking to her because all the tables were busy, and I asked her if I could sit on an empty chair at her table. So, I was seeing the signs all around me, telling me that love was still alive, and that anything was possible as long as I kept an open mind.

I created my online profile, sat down and made a 'love board' as I called it. On it I expressed through words and photos all the experiences I wanted to share with the new relationship I knew was going to come. This represented the values, dreams and desires that I wanted to share with this special person. This became a magnet for my mind to attract the person I wanted to welcome into my life, and I kept adding to it as needed.

Initially, I seemed of interest only to highly intellectual men who felt boring to me. I value intelligence but I also wanted passion and excitement in my life.

As these secondary qualities didn't seem to be available in excess, I added photos that expressed them to attract this energy.

Two months later I met Keith just by chance at Foyle's book store. Today we are happily married and there is no looking back.

Have The Courage To Expand Your Comfort Zone

This only happened to me because I was able to stretch my comfort zone. I was open to talk to a stranger and to let the conversation flow. It's like the chicken eagle that tried once and came back and then tried again and allowed himself to go further, to risk getting lost or even eaten… and it all turned out fine, just because he trusted himself.

Take a look at the diagram below.

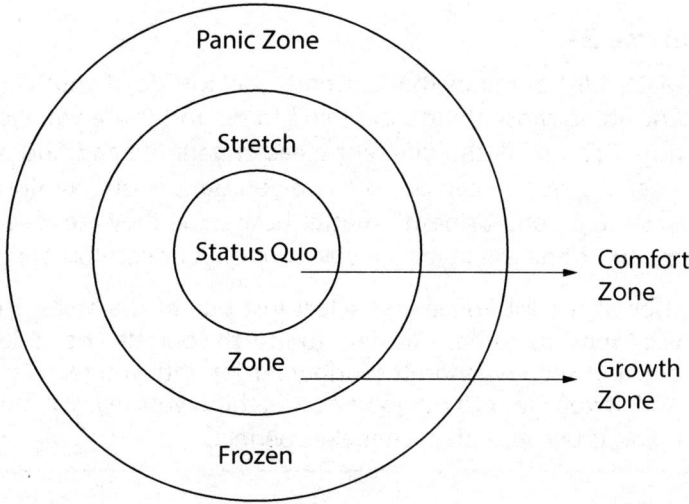

When was the last time you really stepped outside of your comfort zone and tried something new… something that required a little courage? Each time you step out into your 'stretch zone', your comfort zone expands: things that may have paralysed you with fear once now become natural for you. This is when real lasting change in both your personal and professional life takes place. The effort is worth it!

However, there's no need to make big dramatic gestures that might take you out of your stretch zone and into your panic zone, something I often see people doing. This is about trying to find a balance with the unknown. Forcing you to go too far too fast will only be counterproductive – remember the homeostasis principle? So, begin by finding small ways to challenge yourself each day and soon you will have the confidence to make more dramatic changes in your life with ease and flow.

Sadly, most people stay in their comfort zone, living lives of conformity, mediocrity and compliance with social norms and attitudes, deluding themselves that there is a bigger society that will take care of them. The renegades, rebels, radicals and non-conformists are the ones that take control of their lives. These are the ones who change the world and live lives of real passion, purpose and prosperity. You need to make a choice about which zone you want to live in, the panic zone, stuck in the status quo zone, or the stretch zone?

Exercise 21

1. Make a list of things that currently are outside of your comfort zone (including those things you need to do and those you would like to do). Think of all the different areas of your life and find at least five small things you can do to move you out of your comfort zone and to stretch you. It doesn't matter how small they are, because if you haven't done them yet, they are out of your comfort zone!

2. Look at the list above and select just one of the areas, the one you want most to do/have/achieve to stretch yourself! Then select the next one and keep working through your list until you reach the bottom. And, if you want to be good at stretching yourself, you need to keep doing it because practice makes perfect.

Your Notes

When my father was diagnosed with cancer three months before his death, I felt pretty much out of my comfort zone. For a while, I felt in the frozen zone. It happened suddenly and I was not emotionally prepared. My father represented to me strength, a man who was always healthy, never ill, and strong in spite of adversity. His death rocked my life. Before this event, I knew that he was there to support me, emotionally, even though he never believed in me as a woman able to do extraordinary things.

On his map of the world, excellence and courage were reserved only for men. But even with his strong convictions, which meant we disagreed many times and over many things, I had him as a role model. His dedication, his perseverance, his commitment to his family, his endless love for my mother were all values that I learned from him, and for which I'm grateful.

I felt very scared when he died, my roots were shaken. Emotionally, I needed to be strong for my mother and the rest of my family. I felt I needed to grow up fast because now any of my future decisions were completely down to me. I needed to transition from the frozen zone to the stretch zone and then into the comfort zone in a matter of weeks. I had no choice but to accept what was happening and move forward with my life. At least I was alive, so I got on with it, overcoming my fears once more.

But remember, fear also likes to visit you in exciting times. When you make the decision to sell or buy a new home, to find the right place, to make sure you have the finances in place, wondering if this is the right time to move and if it will all work out well in the end.

Or when starting a new job, will you settle in? Will you get on with your colleagues and make new friends? Will your boss be happy with you and offer you opportunities for growth within the company? All these unanswered questions pop up into your mind and remain unanswered until you go through the experience.

Or when you finally start the business that you have always wanted, you are free to create your life, but then there is the fear of making it work, of being able to make ends meet, especially at the beginning when you are just starting out on your path.

Unfortunately, most people walk about failing to recognise their opportunities. But they are all around you, as every time something happens in your life directly or indirectly, you are given a choice, and you can think that things just happen by chance, or you can think that everything happens for a reason, even though it doesn't feel like that at the time. If you look below the surface for the gift and the message, you will be able to reveal its purpose, though discovering this can sometimes take many years!

I believe that nothing happens by chance, that all is perfect as it is, that there are signs and messages to follow if you are willing to be open and have the courage to discover what is hidden. Even situations that at the time feel bad and you wished had never happened. Even when the only thing you are aware of is pain, through time I've been able to discover gifts and feel enriched because I have had these experiences.

Are You A Carrot, An Egg, Or A Coffee Bean?

A young woman went to her mother and complained that her life was too hard and how it seemed to her that as soon as one problem was solved a new one arrived to take its place. The girl did not know how she was going to get through all the troubles and just wanted to give up, so tired was she of fighting and struggling.

Her mother took her to the kitchen and filled three pots with water. These she then placed on the stove and waited for the water in each to boil.

When the water was boiling, into the first pot she dropped carrots, into the second she placed eggs and into the third she poured ground coffee beans.

Without saying a word, she sat down and with her daughter waited, watching the pots until twenty minutes had passed. She then turned off the stove and took out the carrots and placed them in a bowl. Then she scooped out the eggs and placed them in another bowl. Finally, she poured out the coffee and placed it in a bowl.

Turning to her daughter, she said: 'Tell me, what do you see?'

'Carrots, eggs, and coffee,' replied the daughter.

At this, the mother brought her closer and asked her to feel the carrots. She did and found they were soft. Her mother then asked her to take an egg and crack it, which she did, pulling off the shell to find a very hard-boiled centre.

Finally, her mother asked her to sip the coffee. The daughter smiled as she tasted its rich aroma and then asked: 'But what does this mean?'

Her mother explained that each of these objects had faced the same adversity – boiling water – but each had reacted differently. The carrot went in hard and unrelenting but came out soft and weak.

The egg had been fragile, but after sitting in the boiling water, its liquid centre inside had turned hard!

The ground coffee beans were unique, however, because they had changed the water.

'Which are you?' the mother asked her daughter. 'When adversity knocks on your door, how do you respond? Are you a carrot, an egg, or a coffee bean?'

Food for Thought

Which are you?

Like the carrot that seems strong, but with pain and adversity, wilts and becomes soft?

Like the egg with its once fluid centre, but which in the face of adversity – death, financial hardship – though seemingly the same on the outside has become bitter and tough with a stiff spirit and hardened inside?

Or like the coffee bean that actually changes the hot water, the very circumstance that brings the pain?

If you are like the bean, when things are at their worst, you will get better and change the situation around you.

Exercise 22

1. When the hours are the darkest and trials are their greatest, do you lift yourself to another level? How do you handle adversity?
2. When faced with adversity, which areas of your life do you handle best, and which the worst?
3. What makes the difference between the two?
4. What would you need to learn to do differently to be like the coffee beans?
5. How different would your life be if you approached adversity in this way?

Your Notes

Fear Helps You Stand Up For What Matters Most

Fear helps you to examine your commitment so you can discover how much you really want something to happen. So, when you start something new, like a new job, you will experience fear that will test your skills and knowledge, as you feel stretched by the task at hand, standing up when you disagree, choosing to do things differently to everyone else because you care about what matters.

Your values will help you stand up to fear, to do what you know is right, even when there is a threat of losing what you have. You will have things come and go in your life, but you need to live with yourself for the rest of your life.

> **Never compromise your values and principles because the price of this is much higher than any circumstances you are facing #CorporateEscape**

Fear Propels Your Growth!

Every turn in my career has been driven by relationships. As if every person in my life brought a different part of me alive, yearning for a different kind of existence. After living with two workaholics in a row, my life/work balance became a priority. I decided to go self-employed, to re-start my business, so I could make my own choices again and ensure my next relationship was with a man who had intellectual, emotional and spiritual intelligence, and so would be able to enjoy life as well as work. I wanted to find someone who was happy with himself, was well balanced and with whom I had shared common values.

I started also working with associates as a way to open up new opportunities and to stretch my skills and abilities. This also showed me the things I liked doing, and the ones I didn't. This made me more aware about what I wanted to have more, and less of, in this new chapter of my life. For me, love and leadership are intrinsically related because love brings more courage into life than any other experience. This is why I'm clear that leaders who don't relate to people can never be true leaders, they are just people in a position of power. You can't have one without the other, and this applies when leading yourself and your life, as well as others.

Every time I've done some work in a large organisation, I have felt a sense of constraint, a missed opportunity to create something great. This is because people with power and influence often choose the easy route, because they want to be popular instead of standing up for what is needed.

I see employees from the top to the bottom of organisations keeping busy but without much passion or commitment, and instead secretly wanting a way out. For me this is a sad reflection on how the drive for power and profit is killing the human spirit in these organisations, and working its way outwards to help create a valueless and soulless society.

This is another of the reasons for writing this book, to help you awaken and realise that wherever you are in your professional life there are many options and possibilities open to you. I have changed career four times, and by now I know that there is a formula that works every time. In fact I have been giving you the clues all the way through. But don't worry, we will look at this in more detail.

You Have All You Need To Take The Next Step

You really do have all you need to take the next step, but there are three things you need to find out in order to manage change differently and effectively while keeping fear at bay:

1. Your natural change style

2. Your values that will create your drive

3. Your beliefs that will create your strength

Let's look at each in more detail:

1. Discovering Your Natural Change Style

It's very useful to know what is your change readiness, the degree of ease or resistance that you experience in any change situation depending on your natural change preference. Do you prefer order? or do you thrive in chaos?

When working with clients in our programmes, I like to measure their change style and readiness at the start, as it helps us both to know the level of energy they have available for change and their level of openness or resistance to change. This makes it easier to put the right support in place and help them get better results with less pain.

We have already talked about how people like stability, and how when you find this you try to hold on to it as much as possible, even when things are no longer working out. Again, remember the homeostasis principle.

This means that you will resist change until your old ways are no longer effective and something happens that forces you to find new solutions to resolve old problems. Yes, you will resist change and as we have seen this is natural, but you can help yourself by learning how to thrive through change like the Eagle adapting to all of life's seasons.

Why bother? Because if you do this you will be living a very different life, the one you want!

> **Action Step**
>
> Go to **www.maitebaron.com/resourcepack** where you will find a bonus exercise for this section in the online Resources Pack.

Change is as simple or complex as the context, the situation, the external and internal conditions in which it exists. It is affected by your way of thinking and whether you perceive change as an opportunity or as a threat. It will also be influenced by your own past experiences of change; your emotional resilience; the specific moment in your life when the event occurs; the amount of energy you have available for change at a given time; your level of openness or resistance towards what is happening; and your readiness to accept and incorporate new methods, approaches and ideas.

There are a number of areas and several variables that need to be taken into account, as you can't always control external events.

The skills to develop here are agility, adaptability and flexibility to deal with change as a natural event in your life #CorporateEscape

Action Step

Before we carry on, you need to find out more about your own natural change preference style so you will be better able to deal with change right now, because in today's fast moving world, disruptive change can happen in an instant.

So, go to www.maitebaron.com/mychangestyle and join us in one of our webinars to find out more.

After doing this, you will be ready to deal with change differently, more positively, more effectively, so you can make the most of the circumstances you find yourself in and create a lifelong return on your investment.

To take control of your life you need to learn how to take action, so let the real case studies you will find on this page inspire you.

Now that we have looked at your natural change style, let's find out about your values.

2. Discovering Values That Will Drive You

Knowing your values is crucial to designing the next chapter of your life.

For me, in order to know that I'm living *my* life I need to have present: love, passion, fulfillment, learning, health, growth, integrity, courage, contribution and making a difference to others. If these things are not in place, then I feel that something important is missing and I become unsettled. Such uneasiness and lack of flow in my life is a sign that there is an imbalance somewhere.

> **Exercise 23**
>
> If you are feeling this imbalance, then it's time to take stock and re-evaluate where you are in your life, what you are doing and why right now. You can start working this out by writing down:
>
> 1. What matters to you? What are the 'things' you care about in your life?
> 2. What needs to be present in your life for you to know you are living your life? What is not negotiable?

Your Notes

Now that we have looked at your natural change style and the values that create drive for you, it's time to find out more about your beliefs.

3. Discovering The Beliefs That Will Be Your Strength

The beliefs you hold about yourself, your life and what is possible for you and others determines how successful you are in living your life. We have already looked at the importance that your paradigms have had so far in your life's trajectory, so now it's time to become aware of the beliefs you hold, both the ones that empower you, and the ones that are stopping you from growing and becoming who you are born to become.

> **Action Step**
>
> Go **www.maitebaron.com/resourcepack** for bonus exercises for this section in your online pack.

> **Exercise 24**
>
> Write down your beliefs:
>
> 1. What do you believe about yourself?
> 2. What do you believe about work?
> 3. What do you believe about relationships?
> 4. From these lists of beliefs, circle in one colour those that are empowering – they make you feel good about yourself and your life.
> 5. Then circle in another colour your limiting beliefs – those that don't make you feel good.
> 6. Ask yourself, what is the opposite of each limiting belief? Write your answer down next to it.
> 7. Then ask, what needs to happen for me to be able to believe this new belief instead?

Your Notes

Your Life Experience Is Valuable

You are wherever you are in your life right now for a reason and whatever you have learned from all your experiences on your journey so far will allow you to do things differently now, if you chose to.

But often it seems that you need to commit the same mistakes several times for you to fully understand what is going on. You think you have learned a lesson but then you forget it, until the day when everything clicks into place and makes sense.

Even things that didn't work out offer useful lessons, as they provide a contrast that enables you to make comparisons between how life was, and how it is now. This allows you to measure whether things are getting better or worse, whether you are closer or further away from the experience you want to create. Knowing this allows you to adjust your actions as you go along, as well as helping develop your skills.

When you are living a rat-race lifestyle you don't notice these changes because you are having to move so fast that you don't even know where you are. This means it's important for you to create moments of quietness to observe what is going on in your life.

Learn From The Past, Then Let It Go

Throughout time you have made mistakes, everyone has, and you will do so in the future.

Whatever happened has happened, so view each error as a lesson, extracting the wisdom from it and then letting go the feelings you attach to it, because feeding these negative experiences and reliving past mistakes will only take up far too much energy. Focus instead on where you are going, not on where you have come from. The past is gone, let it go, and leave it where it belongs.

To do this requires practice to train your mind for success by giving your unconscious mind clear, concise and consistent instructions. This takes discipline, but persist, because constant practice leads to mastery.

So, beware in the future that every time you talk about frustrating experiences, you are bringing them into the present when they actually should be left in the past.

Fear Is An Emotion Of The Future.
It Only Comes When You Leave The 'Here' And 'Now'

Your mind is incredibly smart, but it can only do one thing at a time. So, you can't be in the present, or the past, or the future all at once.

Unfortunately you either live most of your life in the past, remembering how good or bad things were and noticing how the price of milk and bread has increased, and how now your kids can't play in the street. Or you are most of your time in the future, always running, rushing between your 'to do' lists, feeling that there is never enough time, feeling drained and exhausted and complaining that there is only one you, and not enough hours during the day to 'do' it all.

My diary used to be packed, and if there was any free space, even at the weekend, I needed to fill it. Travelling with me was a nightmare, as I needed to see everything, which meant that a weekend abroad became a sightseeing marathon, so by the Sunday night I was even more exhausted than before. Back then I couldn't appreciate the value of the little things, the experiences that create precious moments that I would savour for years to come. Now, I don't mind where I am, I want to be present, enjoying what I'm doing, so the number of things that I do matters far less, as long as I enjoy what I do.

How do you know if you are in the past or in the future?

If you are in the past there is a feeling of melancholia and of dormancy. If you are in the future then there is a feeling of restlessness, of speed, of never having, doing and being enough. Then fear creeps in, what if I don't do this? What if this is missing? What if it's not good enough?

The beauty of the present is that you can take things for what they are and then decide what to do about them. When you are in the present, things seem to have a different level of urgency and you are able to deal with what comes along in a much calmer way that often turns out to be more effective and efficient anyway. The present allows you to settle things down, to have the time to process and then to make an informed decision.

It was only when both of my parents died that I looked back at the precious moments we had shared, and felt a sense of regret at not having spent more time with them in my 30s, when I was too busy, with my mind in the future, creating my life. Well, these precious moments are the most valuable of my life, the moments I spend with my loved ones, talking with my friends over a glass of wine, sharing our dreams and projects, supporting each other's growth. These moments are the ones you can't buy, the ones that no commercial, shop, role model or corporate position can give you. This is the biggest gift of all: living in the present.

Learn To Slow Down

You can only take quality decisions by being in the present. When you are in a hurry, it's a sign that you are in the future. Notice this fact and draw yourself back to the present. Below is a technique to help you be in the present.

Exercise 25

Technique 1: Focus Fully On Your Breathing

1. Start by noticing your breathing. Put your focus of attention fully on this. Notice how your breathing will start to slow down as you do so and become aware of its pace and how you inhale and exhale. Listen to the sound you produce as well.

2. Slowly become aware of how the things around you begin to look more vivid and clearer. How your sense of time has changed, how all feels slower. Now you are in the 'here and now'.

3. Enjoy this moment of being present, fully feeling the moment.

4. Try to maintain this state for as long as possible.

This little exercise requires practice, and I don't mean once a year, I mean several times a day. This initial effort is worth it, and even if you just do it once a day, quickly it will become more natural.

Your Notes

N.B. There are more bonus techniques for this section in your Resources Pack online. Go to: www.maitebaron.com/resourcepack

How Can You Learn To Deal With Fear With Ease And Confidence?
Fear Disappears When You Stop Feeding It!

Through habit it is all too easy to let your mind focus on what might not work or might not happen rather than focusing your attention positively on what you want to happen.

Fortunately, it is easy to begin to train your mind for success so that you notice what you have, what is working, how lucky you are just by waking up alive every morning, on being healthy, at least more so than others. Then your life will become what you focus on.

> ### Action Step
> Training your mind to be positive is a matter of disciplining yourself to make the right choices. So, every time you find your mind wandering on what doesn't work, flip a coin, and consciously notice how much you have going on for you in your life. Feel grateful.
>
> As it was when we talked about **The *SUPER–* and The *SUPER +* Generation™**, at any given time you can chose to flip a coin and choose whether you want be positive 'heads' or negative 'tails' and then act accordingly.

Your Notes

Some of these techniques may seem complicated to use at first, but actually they are easy and simple to learn and do. So, keep practicing them until they become natural and then you will start using them unconsciously. It's incredibly liberating to be able to move through your life knowing that you can face whatever comes along with ease and confidence.

Key Ideas To Take Away

1. You need to make a choice, to decide to stretch your comfort zone or to stay 'playing small' for the rest of your days. Take little steps until you build the muscle and the confidence you need to stretch yourself more. Remember, practice creates mastery!

2. Your natural ability and agility to deal with change, your values and your beliefs are your inner drive, the motivator and the inner source that controls the quality of your life. You need to understand your change preferences, how open you are to change, what matters to you and how to support yourself better in order to take control of your life.

3. Your skills are transferable between different contexts. Learning new skills, travelling, speaking different languages, doing the same things another way will stretch your mind by developing new pathways that will improve your decision making, your problem solving abilities, your creative and innovative thinking, your flexibility when dealing with challenges and above all keep your brain younger and fitter.

4. Fear can only appear in the future. By learning how to be in the present, not only will you enjoy life much more but you will also keep fear away. We looked at how to practice being in the present by focusing fully on your breathing.

N.B. There are more bonus techniques on how to be in the present in your Resources Pack online. Go to: www.maitebaron.com/resourcepack

In Chapter 7, you will learn…

How the past doesn't equal the future and how at any given time you have the right to take a different path. How you need to update and expand your vision in a world that is constantly in flux. Why today you need to revisit your professional direction and take new decisions, because what used to be the safest option has become a threat if you want be in control of your life and destiny.

You will learn the steps to create your own *Corporate Escape System*™: **7 Steps To Become A New Entrepreneur** and how to face and overcome the seven most common excuses that will keep you stuck in this frantic and pointless rat race. The chapter finishes with a redefinition of success in the full sense of the word.

So keep reading… there are plenty of life-changing suggestions and strategies in the pages to come. By now you probably know or are close to guessing what is the secret theme beyond the theme. Is this the case for you?

Chapter 7

Today Is The First Day Of The Rest Of Your Life To Start Afresh

*The Past Doesn't Equal The Future.
Today Is A New Beginning*

Decide First Then Commit

I often work though the concepts and information contained in this book with clients, and they tell me that they wish that someone had explained all this to them many years ago.

And one thing that is always of great interest is helping them distinguish between making a decision and committing to something.

At any given time you make decisions you believe are best based on the information you have at the time. However, can you think of a time when you were offered something, a contract, a job, or an assignment? You felt so flattered by the offer that you said 'yes' straight away, without taking the time to think through whether this was right for you?

You said 'yes', and you were sucked in.

Then, what was meant to last three months became six, and then a year and then two. Before you knew it, your 'yes' had become your life. This happens with jobs, relationships and friendships... and before you realise your world has become taken over by things and people who don't matter to you, and who are not aligned with your core values, and who are often just thinking about themselves.

So, be clear about this distinction, you need to decide first, then commit. But to be able to do this, you need to know what you want, and how saying 'yes' will feel for you. Learn to 'feel' this 'yes' in your body. How will your body feel doing this project? What will be your energy level at the end of the day doing this job? Does this idea fit with your plan? Would this decision get you closer or further away from your life vision?

Follow your gut instinct and nurture your intuition, these are gifts given to you, for a reason. Remember that your unconscious mind's job is to support you to achieve fulfillment. The more connection there is between your mind-body-spirit the easier it will be for you to access the wisdom of all your **seven CEOs**. A well developed intuition (your 5th CEO) will allow you to notice very small subtle sensations in your body, which will translate into thoughts that give you inner messages.

So, start developing your intuition, learning how to listen to it more. A simple way of doing this is to notice the first sensation, thought, whatever comes initially when you meet a new person. Do you trust them? Do you feel connected? Is there something inside you telling you to be cautious? You are doing this all the time, even when you are not aware of it. The skill is how to become aware of your intuition while everything else is going on.

Action Step
To be able to tune in more and more with your intuition you need to become aware first of your gut instinct, when and how it's telling you something is right, and when it's not. Keep notes about these experiences, review them regularly and learn from them.

You Need To Engage With Your Life

If your job or career doesn't feel right for you, accept this and ask yourself: What do I want to do about it?

Don't waste another ten years, hoping that things will change and get better because in all probability they won't. Take responsibility, face up to your fear and act; even just a small step such as making a list of the things you would rather be doing is better than doing nothing. As soon as you put your mind to work you have already begun your next journey. Remember, your mind works with images and through repetition.

How many times have you heard people saying: *'when I retire then I will...'*

Well, I hope that by now you already know that this never works, especially nowadays when the idea of retiring at all is an ever distant prospect. The perfect time to change your situation is now; in fact it's the only thing you can do for sure.

If you are unhappy with your relationship, be open about it. If there is hope, give it a second chance, but only for a specific time, then reassess and decide. One of the most challenging things to accept in life is that whatever is not there, just is not there.

Do you know of anybody who has been in an unfulfilling relationship for many years, just hoping that things will change? I do. In fact, I have done this twice myself, each time using up ten years of my life focusing on the wrong person. I'm naturally an optimist and a strong believer in human excellence so I used to fall in love with the future manifestation of the person, not with the present human being who was in front of me. I could see their greatness, what they might achieve, their potential… what I didn't want to accept is that some people don't want to be great, they are happy being ordinary, just going through the motions, without ever reaching their potential because they choose not to.

This is a big lesson to learn. Some people in your life will be ready to take the leap, to grow, to stretch themselves, and others will be dominated by their fears forever. So, it's natural to leave people that you connected with in the past, in the past. When they don't want to live in the present or future you want to create for yourself, it's time to let it go. Choose people and experiences that make you flourish and let go of the rest!

This is not being selfish. You can't force others to achieve their potential if they don't want to. At the same time, if you have the desire and the ambition to become the best you can be during your lifetime, you can't stop doing it just because others don't want to follow you.

The likelihood is that if you do this with your relationships you also have the same approach at work. It's easy to believe that: 'Things will be better when the new CEO comes along; or when the new department opens; or when the IT is upgraded.' But time passes, and you end up working longer hours, that affect your health and your relationships, perhaps with somebody who doesn't care.

Before I divorced, I realised that either I had to face my fear and go, or sink together with him because he didn't want to grow, he was stuck in the past and I wasn't. I wanted to feel alive again and to live my life to the full. He became an obstacle wanting to stop me from becoming me. I had no choice. I chose my life.

Have you ever made sacrifices in the name of love? I imagine so. I have come to realise that where there is true love, there are no sacrifices to be made, there is space for respecting what you both want, so supporting each other's growth is at the core of the relationship. It's a natural dance where sometimes you take, and sometimes you give.

I could say, 'If I had only known this a few years back', but that would be nonsense, I needed to go through these experiences to know the difference. So, I'm grateful for my past, it has been perfect for getting me to where I am today. If you think about it, your past has been perfect for you too. Can you see this? But the past is gone, and the present is here, with new opportunities and challenges to be conquered and seized. Your past has just equipped you for what is next…

The Future Of Work… If You Had A Crystal Ball

Things Are Different Today, Open Your Eyes

A few generations back, even until the last few years, the idea of working for somebody else, especially a big organisation, was seen as the more secure option. Unfortunately, millions of people today still cling to this idea as a solution, hoping and expecting that somebody will give them a job. The reality is that this expectation is unfounded and surreal in today's fast-changing world.

Let's look at why today it is riskier to work for an organisation than it is to work for yourself.

1. Unemployment is rising in most industrialised countries. The painful truth here is that there are more people looking for a job then there are job vacancies available.

2. The number of redundancies is expected to increase, as companies downsize and machinery replaces more and more jobs. Do you know that today the US uses only 10% of the workforce that China uses to produce the same amount of goods? And as machines become better still, the number of people needed will decrease further.

3. Technology has made outsourcing very accessible to all, which means that even the self-employed can enjoy technical support that previously was only available to big companies. The downside is that organisations can also find very experienced professionals at a fraction of the cost of what they are paying you now as a salaried employee.

4. The use of the internet and mobile technology has expanded the marketplace, creating access to a gigantic pool of potential clients. Today you can test an idea and launch a new business for very little money. And, as the technology becomes easier and faster, this will become much more broadly available and better.

5. People are tired of the same old stuff and are looking for more specialised and distinctive products and services. But organisations are stuck with their bureaucracy and long-winded decision processes. This weakens their position in the market, giving smaller and more flexible companies a competitive advantage.

6. The retirement age keeps sliding up, so job satisfaction is becoming more important than ever. If you're going to need to carry on working into at least your 70s, isn't it worth doing something you love? This fact is shifting people's perceptions and making them ever more unwilling to put their life on hold forever.

7. The impact on the health of those working in organisations is beyond belief, with the incidence of stress and depression on the rise. This is good news for pharmaceutical companies who will carry on growing without a second thought about the role they are playing in all of this. Considering that there will be fewer people because of redundancies and improved technologies, and the robots to come (it's not science fiction, think about how car manufacturing has changed), the life/work balance of the workforce will just get worse and worse.

8. Today it is easier than ever before to get together with a group of people to source different skills and create something new. This means your skills can be leveraged much faster, and in a way that is not possible inside the corporate world due to internal politics, rigid structures and policies. So, you can spend the rest of your life killing yourself going up the career ladder or you can create a ladder for yourself and go up that at your own pace in your own way, on your own or with a group of dynamic like-minded professionals.

9. Corporations are older and heavier than dinosaurs. They carry a lot of baggage and are full of old ideas, rigidity and narrow-mindedness and offer 20th century solutions to a 21st century world. Creativity and innovation are much more likely to come from small businesses that are more entrepreneurial, faster and more agile. Small businesses may look weak today but they will become stronger and bigger. The existing model of the big organisations is in decline and it's just a matter of time until it becomes extinct altogether.

10. Organisations believe they own you, and with the technology currently available they expect you to be available 24/7. Well I don't know about you, but I love what I do and also have a rich personal life that is important to me, so I'm not willing to trade my life/work balance and the fulfillment of my life for their dreams of profit. They don't care about my health and satisfaction, but I do and I hope you care about yours because your life is precious!

Let's Redefine Success

The way you see the world and what you notice or fail to notice about it will impact the way you go through your life. You are born with everything you need to create an amazing experience, it's therefore up to you to learn how to use what is given to you to the best of your abilities so as to create the results you want for yourself and others. People you see as more successful may not have had any more advantages than you at their birth, and perhaps even fewer. So it's your desire to succeed, your commitment to a cause you believe in that will shape your destiny and help you overcome any obstacles.

Let me tell you a story.

What Do You Perceive As The Seven Wonders Of The World?

A group of students were asked to list what they thought were today's 'Seven Wonders of the World'. Though there were disagreements, they eventually voted for the following:

1. Egypt's Great Pyramids
2. The Taj Mahal
3. The Grand Canyon
4. The Panama Canal
5. The Empire State Building
6. St. Peter's Basilica
7. The Great Wall of China

While gathering the votes, the teacher noticed that one quiet student hadn't yet turned in her list, so she asked the girl if she was having trouble deciding what to choose.

'Yes,' said the girl, 'a little. I couldn't make up my mind because there were so many.'

'Well,' said her teacher, 'tell us what you have, and maybe we can help you decide.'

The girl hesitated and then read from her list:

'I think the 'Seven Wonders of the World' are:

1. To see
2. To hear
3. To touch
4. To taste
5. To feel
6. To laugh
7. And to love.'

The room was so quiet you could have heard a pin drop.

And the moral of this story?

The things we overlook as simple and ordinary and that we take for granted are often truly wondrous and cannot be built by hand or bought by man.

Your Notes

....

....

....

....

If you are reading this book, then you were given the gift of a pair of eyes to see and to create a vision for your life. If you can hear the birds outside your window, then you also have a pair of ears to listen to others, to nature and to music. If you can feel the sunshine warming your skin, then you have an amazing working body to move you around from one place to the next. If you are aware of your thoughts, then you also have a functioning mind.

> **One skill to acquire is the ability to succeed in life by making the most of what you are given, on your own terms #CorporateEscape**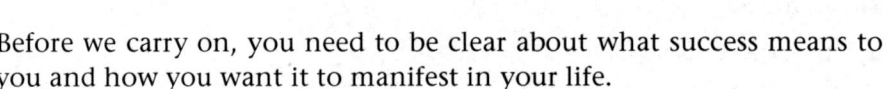

Before we carry on, you need to be clear about what success means to you and how you want it to manifest in your life.

You already know that having a career, a car, a house or two, money in the bank may seem like success to most, but unless your life makes sense and you feel happy with yourself and your life as a whole, this may not feel much like success to you.

And of course, there are as many definitions of success as people in the world, so you need to create your own.

There is no formula to define success. There is no right or wrong to this, there are no absolutes, it's just what feels right or not, for you. You are the one that must take the many possible ingredients that create success and bring them together in your own recipe, and just to get you started, here's mine.

For me, success means living my life in harmony and balance within the different areas of my life, while being self-sufficient and contributing to others to make the world a better place.

So let's find out what success means for you.

> **Exercise 26**
>
> This is a short version of an exercise you can find in more detail in your Resources Pack online by going to: **www.maitebaron.com/resourcepack**
>
> Answer the questions about success.
>
> 1. What does success look like and feel like to you in *financial terms?*
> 2. What does success look like and feel like to you in terms of *emotional wellbeing?*
> 3. What does success look like and feel like to you in terms of *relational fulfillment?*
> 4. What does success look like and feel like to you in terms of *physical health and fitness?*
> 5. What does success look like and feel like to you in terms of *spiritual fulfillment?*

Your Notes

Until now, probably you have being defining success mostly in terms of your career and your financial rewards, doing plenty of things you don't want to do or aren't passionate about just to pay your mortgage.

Today, I invite you to redefine success in your life taking into account all of these five aspects: financially, emotionally, relationally, physically, spiritually.

If you create a broader vision for your life as a whole and how to fulfill all these parts of you, you will feel more at peace, alive and happy. You will be able to live more in the present, without the need to escape to the past or future, because your current reality will be so rewarding and rich, that will be more than enough. The urge to have more for the sake of it will disappear.

As I mentioned at the beginning, you are given everything you need to create what you want in the way that you desire. So let's see how you can maximise these birth gifts in a manner that will support your plans and dreams to achieve a life of success in the fullest sense.

Become More Adaptable And Flexible To Thrive Through Change

At the end of the day, you are faced with one major choice: to live your life or to live someone else's. It's as crude and simple as this. This decision, as you well know now, is very important because it will affect the quality of the relationships you have, the way you work and with whom, the friendships you have, the people you surround yourself with or where you go on holidays... every single aspect of every important choice in your life.

But unless you are willing to overcome your limiting beliefs about what is possible for you, to do what it takes to expand your mind, to shift your paradigms and to change the habits and routines that don't support you, you won't be able to create the life you want. You will not become more adaptable or better able to thrive through change and so you will be faced with the risk of being left behind.

As Darwin said more than 100 years ago: 'It's not the strongest that survive nor the most intelligent. It is the ones who are most adaptable to change that survive.' On which side are you today?

Creating a Plan B, Starting Today
You Choose *Your* Life Or Someone Else's

But before you move on, just stop for a moment, and imagine that you are ninety years old sitting in the comfy chair of your beloved living room taking stock of an empty life simply because you had chosen to do nothing with it. Feel the regrets, the heaviness of wasted time, the sadness that comes from not doing the things you wanted to because you never really felt alive. The fear kept creeping in and you only 'played small' because you didn't have the courage to face it and so never made the effort to self-develop and grow into the person you could have been.

I hope that these thoughts scare you to the point of taking action! So now, go ahead, make a plan to change what needs to be changed and to take conscious actions to take control of your life, because nobody else will or can do it for you.

> *What I'm suggesting is not that you hand in your resignation without knowing what to do next. What I'm inviting you to do is to begin to create a plan B that puts things in place so you can make a decision at any time, knowing that you have an alternative plan, with all the puzzle pieces together, and in place, to make it happen*

The Corporate Escape System™:
The Corporate Escape Accelerated Programme: 7 Steps To Become A New Entrepreneur™

I'm happy to share with you our flagship Accelerated Programme. This is the programme I take my clients through to help them achieve the powerful breakthroughs that will give them a competitive advantage efficiently and effectively, achieving results much faster than any other way I know.

It's a process that contains seven steps to help you **Escape *and* Succeed Beyond the Corporate Walls by Becoming a New Entrepreneur™**. You can get started on your own using all the bonuses and resources available to you online or you can choose to join us to get even greater results. Having support in place will keep you focused while holding you more accountable to yourself and others. Sometimes this can be scary and, as you well know by now, fear will try to pull you back and keep you where you are. But with support from others who are in the same boat you can become a pivotal ingredient in your own success.

The Corporate Escape Accelerated Programme: **7 Steps To Become A New Entrepreneur™** provides a strong foundation for those who want to escape the corporate walls and to succeed on their terms. It is also perfect for those professionals who are already outside the corporate constraints trying to work out what to do next and how to make that happen.

This group includes professionals who have already been made redundant, those who are between jobs and careers, wanting to start their own business, and even small business owners who need to get to the next level but don't know how.

This Programme Has Three Main Objectives:

1. To Help You Be Fit And Ready For Whatever Comes Your Way. We have seen how uncertainty is the only certain thing and how not doing anything to take control of your life puts you more at risk. Creating a plan B doesn't commit you to do anything until you want to, but it does give you a competitive advantage that will place you well above other professionals competing for your job and who are not preparing themselves for the changes to come.

We enable professionals to break free from conformity and mediocrity so that they can live a life in which they embrace their passion and purpose so they bring prosperity to their lives.

Getting clarity, purpose and direction to move forward with your life is a must.

2. **To Help You Succeed Beyond Corporate So That You Can Find An Alternative Way Of Working** that doesn't force you to go back to the corporate world if you don't want to.

The Corporate Escape Accelerated Programme: **7 Steps To Become A New Entrepreneur™** gives professionals like you the knowledge and skills you need to build your vision in a way that will help you achieve success on your terms and in a way that feels meaningful to you.

3. **It Will Help You Build Your Emotional Resilience So That You Are Ready To Face Whatever Comes Along,** leaving uncertainty, confusion and fear behind. Through this programme you will **evolve professionally and personally** in an exponential and generative way. Its ripple effect is one of the extra bonuses of this programme because you'll experience the benefits not just in one area of your life but in many, and in a way that will have a positive impact not only for you but those around you. The purpose of this is to help you live with passion, purpose and prosperity by achieving emotional, financial, physical, relational and spiritual fulfillment in a way that you haven't experienced before.

> *The real escape doesn't happen until you update your mindset and leave your old constraints and limitations behind! #CorporateEscape*

We have looked at how crucial it is to shift your mindset as well as updating your limiting beliefs and the paradigms that have kept you stuck. Through this programme you will undertake a number of assessments that will help you to go far beyond your current level of awareness about yourself, your talents, your belief system, your readiness to change, your values system and the world around you, both its challenges and opportunities. This will enable you to understand which are the areas you need to work on most to get ready to escape the corporate rat race and succeed beyond, on your own terms.

This powerful journey to becoming a New Entrepreneur will also help you develop the skills you need to succeed in today's world and will support you through the implementation process.

Right now you are either still stuck inside looking forward to escape, or outside, confused and uncertain about what to do next.

So let's see what can be done...

The Corporate Escape Accelerated Programme: 7 Steps To Become A New Entrepreneur™ is based on the acronym **C.O.U.R.A.G.E.**, which describes a clear step-by-step process that allows you to achieve consistent high quality results.

Let's look at each step in turn.

1. C is for Clarity of *Vision and Direction*

Here the objective is to become clear about where you are now; who you are; what you stand for; what is important to you; what you want; and how you manage change. Throughout the book I have included several exercises to help you get started with all this. Revisit them if you need to.

By the end of this module you will know your mission, your vision, your values, your life purpose, as well as how you can start adjusting to the major changes you need to make in your professional and personal life. This gives a strong foundation to build your future on.

2. O is for Opportunities and Obstacles: *Acknowledge and Accept*

In this module you will find out what you are good at, what you love doing and how this will help you to create a viable business. It's crucial to have answers to all three of these questions. To do this you need to explore your skills, gifts, talents, strengths, knowledge, experience as well as your weaknesses and potential areas for development. This will help you decide which of these you can outsource and which you need to learn more about. This is about how to leverage all that you already know and are good at.

3. U is for YOU: *Unleash Your Potential With A Powerful Mindset*

This is a life-changing module because it's all about the inner-YOU. Here we look at your mindsets, your beliefs, your paradigms, your emotional blockages, your energy drains, your money leaks and your world views. The aim here is to build emotional resilience, expand your mind and shift your mindsets. Going from employment to becoming a New Entrepreneur is a big mindset shift that can't be ignored or overlooked and is, I believe, by far the main reason for failure among start-up entrepreneurs and small business owners. This module is transformational and from this moment on you will feel better about your life and the opportunities you have ahead.

Do you remember that you can't make deep lasting change without shifting your mindsets and your identity first? Unfortunately this is what a lot of quick-fix programmes try to do, but ignoring the importance of this just results in a waste of time, money and energy, which will make you feel even more frustrated and keep you stuck. I believe in doing quality work that will develop your sense of identity and skills for life, and there is nothing more valuable than working on yourself, as this is the greatest return on investment for life, both personally and professionally.

I'm not interested in working with people 'just because'. I'm passionate about developing New Entrepreneurs, Eagles who want to take responsibility for their own life's success and are willing to fly by living with passion, purpose and prosperity so they can create social change and make the world a better place. For this you need a sound foundation and this is what I deliver!

We have too many Chickens in the world and not enough Eagles. I'm looking to change this. Remember the chicken eagle? You need to choose on which side you want to be. If you choose to be an Eagle then you need to go through the process of change like the bird at the start of the book, it's your choice. And I'm here to support you in this journey if this is what you want.

4. R is for Road Map

Once the groundwork is done and you have deep answers about yourself, your vision and what you want, we will look at how you are going to make this happen and then encapsulate this in a step-by-step road map with milestones to measure your progress and success.

This is a powerful step-by-step process to help you get clarity, direction and create a good balance by applying the new concepts you have learned as building blocks for your new business. At this stage you will be well equipped to succeed in the brave 'new' professional world.

5. **A is for Ask for Help and Support:** *Relationships & Collaboration*

This module is about collaboration because nobody can succeed alone, something that you have heard thousands of times because it's true. So, here you will work out the resources that you need; the skills that you either have, need to acquire or outsource; how social media, partnership and joint ventures can help you; and how you can build the right team to support you.

6. **G is for Goals and Greater Good**

Next we start to look at your life through a broader lens that will help you determine the legacy that you want to leave behind. You are here to leave a legacy whether you like it or not. You are more than just an ant; remember the beginning of the book? And you will leave a legacy, no matter what, because everything you do has an impact, directly or indirectly, on others.

We are all interconnected so you need to choose consciously what you want to leave behind. Otherwise you may find when the time comes that it's too late and all that you can leave is a small imprint that doesn't make you feel great because it lacks your personality, your uniqueness and your greatness. It's a legacy, but one that just shows the world that you didn't fulfil your life purpose when you had the chance.

Most leaders don't think about this at all, but making this decision will give you focus, purpose and strength in a way you don't know is available to you. This is a responsibility and a choice that New Entrepreneurs can and need to wholeheartedly embrace.

7. **E is for Energise Your Life:** *Engage with yourself and others*

Here we will create a plan to help you achieve the life/work balance you need and want. And yes, you do need to plan this, otherwise some areas of your life will be out of balance. So, you need to be clear about how you are going to manage your energy and keep healthy and fit; and determine when it's working time or family time or time for 'you'.

This is about creating a lifestyle plan, where there is space for all the eight main areas of your life, all working together and sustaining each other in harmony. Can you imagine how different your life will be then?

> **This is an exciting journey, but it is one that is not for everybody. You will feel excited about this opportunity if you are willing to take control of your life, if you are frustrated enough, if you are willing to take charge and if you have the courage to do what you are born to do**

> **Today being an employee is riskier than working for yourself. The time has come to become a New Entrepreneur #CorporateEscape**

Action Step

Get started by taking our free 'Your Life Success Assessment: Discover The Naked Truth About 8 Key Areas Of Your Life' at

www.maitebaron.com/lifesuccessassessment

Excuses Will Not Get You Out And Will Not Help You Eat

By now you know that the natural human reaction is to keep repeating what you are doing so as to preserve your perceived security. You also know that your mind will create plenty of excuses to preserve the status quo.

But at the end of the day it's your life, so you can choose to drown in your own excuses or to be brave and at least explore your life's possibilities by finding your own answers to each of the seven **COURAGE** steps mentioned above. You don't need to make any commitment to anything, just be open and see what else could be possible. Or better still, join us so we can explore together and decide later on what you want to do: it's up to you if you decide to stay or to leave.

Certainly making this transition does require being prepared and unfortunately most professionals don't get professional help to get ready, so if redundancy suddenly strikes they get in pretty bad shape, pretty quickly. Today you are being given a chance to get ready for whatever may come.

So, take responsibility for your life, start preparing your plan B and don't be like those who use the many excuses I'm about to describe for doing nothing, some of which will push your buttons and make you feel uncomfortable.

Of course, you may ask yourself, who is she to tell me that this is not true?

I'm not telling you if it's true or not, what I'm doing is giving you the opportunity to look at all these excuses as an objective observer to see the level of truth for yourself

See this as an opportunity to be honest with yourself, a moment to quietly reflect on your life, what is going well and what you would like to be different; you will feel more open to explore other possibilities and find a way out.

Remember, you can lie to the world forever, but you can't lie to yourself.

> **Action Step**
> Look at the excuses below and see how many you sometimes, occasionally or frequently use. Write 'Yes' next to each one. This will help create a picture of your thinking right now and will make you more aware of what needs to be different if you want to create different results.

Excuse 1: Wrong Timing: *'Now is the wrong time.'*

'With unemployment rising, uncertainty about the housing market and interest rates and the global financial situation, I can't take the risk right now and make changes. Perhaps in a few years time when everything's more stable I will.'

The truth is there never is a perfect time to make changes. If you decide to wait and then you're made redundant you will be faced with no choice at all. And, by not taking the responsibility today to create your life the way you want it, you will be wasting valuable time you could be using to get ready, fit and prepared for whatever comes next. So, let's get this right, doing nothing knowing that life-changing circumstances are possible, probable and even in many cases predictably certain, is more irresponsible then looking for other options while you still have some control. Taking action today doesn't mean you need to jump today. It just means that if you need to, or choose to, or have to, you will be ready to fly and soar like the Eagle that on its 40th birthday took the decision to change.

Of course, you might decide that you'll take the risk, and worry about it when the worst happens. But if you do that, in the meantime, your dreams, your hopes, your passions, the real you will become increasingly submerged in a life of apathy, conformity and mediocrity. And this applies not just to your working life, but your relationships, your lifestyle, your health – all will go the same way.

Excuse 2: External Circumstances

For example, *'My daughter is going to university next year so I need to save and keep the ball rolling. It wouldn't be responsible of me to do this and I would feel selfish.'*

Taking on board other's commitments to the detriment of your own may make you feel good about yourself but it creates the perfect excuse for doing nothing about changing your own life. In fact, you are deferring the responsibility of taking control, while encouraging others not to take control of theirs. So, while superficially this may look like a good thing to do and society even values this sort of behavior, it's just another instance of social conformity designed to control your actions.

In the long-run, you are not helping whoever it is, be it your daughter, or someone else. To be a Leader you need to stand up for yourself doing whatever needs to be done and which is right for you. By not doing this, you are turning others into followers for the rest of their lives, hoping that someone else will also take care of their future. You will also be giving up precious years of your life, years that you will never get back. The great thing is that you can have what you want while your daughter, or whoever, gets what they want too and all at the same time. You have to create a win-win situation for you both by creating a plan of action for yourself, and encouraging the other person to do the same for themselves too.

Excuse 3: Wrong Age

Generally this equates to: *'I'm too old'* (although I do hear plenty saying: *'I'm too young'*). Or, *'I'm still at an age when I need to pay the mortgage so now is not the right time to start something new. If it doesn't work I could lose everything I have worked for all my life.'* With this type of excuse you are likely to have a lot of external support to sustain and reinforce this debilitating belief from people who will agree by saying *'You are right. Who, in their mind, would do this at your age?'* *'Precisely,'* you say, *'we all know this is crazy.'*

But what are these voices going to say when your job disappears? Or when some other unforeseen event arrives in your life? Or when you have to sell up at the bottom of the property market? Or when there are no other jobs around and everyone else you know is in a similar situation? These same voices are likely to be saying *'Well you should have prepared for this situation.'*

The fact is that you have no other choice but to do something. You need to take control of your life and it doesn't matter how young or old you are. The nanny state is in decline and *you*, and nobody else but *you*, is responsible for your own survival and success. It's time to stop this well worn social denial that when something feels hard or is an unpleasant truth we should ignore it and pretend it's not real.

Excuse 4: Wrong Set of Skills, Upbringing or Experience

'I'm lucky to have a job right now. Period. With all the technology and all the youngsters competing for my job it's unlikely that I would even get this job now,

so I'm better off where I am, where I don't need to retrain. In any event, to do something different I'd need to have plenty of experience and contacts to be able to make it take off. Anyway, this is what we've always done in my family, and I don't have the right connections or know the right people to succeed, and I didn't go to a well-known university.'

Personally I find this type of excuse exceptionally irritating when you consider that two-thirds of the world's billionaires are self-made and that they have the same 24 hours a day as the rest of us.

Perhaps this excuse might have had some truth to it in the 'old world', but now opportunities are open to anyone living in a civilised country.

Today what does create the big divide is mostly to do with two factors: your attitude towards time and your attitude towards money, and again this is all to do with your mindset!

How do you use your time? Do you waste it spending hours on Facebook or watching YouTube or television, playing online games with no focus or direction? Or, do you invest your time in your education, self-development, learning new skills and travelling to learn from other cultures?

How do you spend your money? Do you waste it buying more clothes than you need, smoking, drinking a bottle of wine every day, taking expensive weekends away here and there, going out every weekend to be entertained, and buying the latest gadgets? Or do you invest it in activities that will bring real return on your investments like in education, self-development and learning new skills?

Excuse 5: Don't Have The Money

'I can't start my own business or change career now, it's too late, I will need extra training and this takes time and money. I can't ask for help because I already have a mortgage, credit card debt and a car loan so money is always going to be an issue. But if I win the lottery then...'

The reality is that today you can start a business on a shoestring budget, and with just an idea, a computer and a mobile phone to make videos, you can go a long way. With millions around the world as your potential client base there are no restrictions as there were before.

If money is an issue, it's because you keep repeating behaviour that make it an issue. Unless you invest in yourself so as to learn about what you are currently doing that doesn't work and to discover how to do things differently, money will always be an issue. Money is a matter of mindset and choice!

I meet people all the time that complain about not having 'enough' money. Then when we start looking at their lifestyle and habits it becomes quite apparent what is going on: what they make, they waste. Worse even, they spend much more than they earn! Often there is no concept of saving or investing money in things that will build up more wealth.

The bottom line here is that you can't have a champagne lifestyle with a lemonade wage!

> **It's quite amazing how well educated we can be in most aspects & how illiterate when it comes to emotions, love and money #CorporateEscape**

Money attitudes are a matter of mindset but the good news is: when you update your money mindset you will change the results you get!

> **I believe that wealth is a birthright; becoming financially independent is an adult's responsibility #CorporateEscape**

Excuse 6: Wrong Identity

'I'm not the successful type. I never did very well at school. I didn't even finish college and certainly didn't go to university. I'm not a born leader or entrepreneur. Of course, it would be nice to be like Richard Branson but success is not for people like me.'

Well, Richard Branson was dyslexic and didn't do well at school; Andre Agassi winner of eight Grand Slam titles quit school in the ninth grade and turned tennis pro at the age of 16; Bill Gates, billionaire co-founder of Microsoft, dropped out of Harvard after his second year to work with Paul Allen on the venture that became Microsoft; Paul Getty, once the richest man in the world, failed to graduate from university; Winston Churchill, rebellious by nature, did poorly in school and flunked sixth grade. He applied to the Royal Military Academy at Sandhurst, but it took him three attempts before he passed the entrance exam. He graduated 8th out of a class of 150 a year and a half later. He never attended college; Paulo Coelho was institutionalised from the age of 17 until he was 20. He later enrolled in law school but dropped out after one year, became a hippie, travelled the world, and then later worked as a songwriter before writing his first novel *The Alchemist* which to date has sold more than 60 million copies.

And the list could go on and on and includes examples from every possible category of life: there are business people, sportsmen and women, artists, singers, politicians and scientists who have had the 'wrong identity', so please do yourself a favour and find a different excuse. With this one you are not likely to get much empathy nor sympathy nowadays, when people from all life avenues are achieving success faster than ever before just by using their talents to the fullest and maximising all the opportunities around.

Excuse 7: Wrong Place

'In my country, city or town these ideas don't work. We are different here you know. We don't like all these rapid changes. We like tradition and to keep things as they are. Here there are not many opportunities, you stick to what you can do and that's it.'

Well, given the reach of internet there are no geographical limits any more, so wherever you come from or live is almost irrelevant. With a computer you are living in the 'perfect' place. Update your skills to use it at its best, that's all it takes.

I would like to see your face now. Do any, some or most of these excuses resonate with you? I imagine that at least one will, but now it's time to get out of whatever trance you are currently in and move on! You need to decide what you want from your life and take action; this is the only thing that can get you different results: *Action*. It's up to you, nothing else or anybody else!

> **Action Step**
> 1. Look at your list of excuses.
> 2. Update your limiting beliefs about each one of them. We looked at how to do this in Chapter 6 and in your Resources Pack online. Go back if you need to. **www.maitebaron.com/resourcepack**
> 3. Update your beliefs and decide what action you want to take for each one of them so as to move forward with your life.

How Can You Make The Most Of Your Life?
Face Whatever You Are Scared Of And Liberate Yourself

We have seen how feeling scared is normal and how your brain will treat with caution any new experiences, concepts, adventures and behaviours. However, by being aware of this you can consciously determine your re-actions and how you will deal with this fear in a way that is empowering instead of debilitating.

But if even the thought of leaving your job, the organisation you have put so much time and effort into, is too scary and daunting, here are 21 things to remember.

21 Things To Remember

1. No one can ruin your day without your permission.
2. Most people will be about as happy as they decide to be.
3. Others can stop you temporarily, but only you can do it permanently.
4. Whatever you are willing to put up with is exactly what you will have.
5. Success stops when you do.
6. When your ship comes in, make sure you are willing to unload it.
7. You will never 'have it all together'.
8. Life is a journey… not a destination. Enjoy the trip!
9. The biggest lie on the planet: 'When I get what I want, I will be happy.'
10. The best way to escape your problem is to solve it.
11. I've learned that ultimately, 'takers' lose and 'givers' win.
12. Life's precious moments don't have value, unless they are shared.
13. If you don't start, it's certain you won't arrive.
14. We often fear the thing we want the most.
15. He or she who laughs… lasts.
16. Yesterday was the deadline for all complaints.
17. Look for opportunities… not guarantees.
18. Life is what's coming… not what was.
19. Success is getting up one more time.
20. Now is the most interesting time of all.
21. When things go wrong… don't go with them.

Your Notes

> *"The future has several names.*
> *For the weak, it is impossible.*
> *For the fainthearted, it is unknown.*
> *For the thoughtful and valiant, it is ideal."*
>
> Victor Hugo

Key Ideas To Take Away

1. You need to redefine success on your terms. I invite you take into account these five aspects: financial, emotional, physical, relational and spiritual so that you are able to experience success in its fullest sense in each and every area of your life. You can live with passion, purpose and prosperity, don't settle for less!
2. At any given time you can start afresh. Your past is just a guide. Your present is what matters, and only by taking decisive action will you be able to create the future you want.
3. The seven most common excuses that people keep repeating to themselves which keep them stuck in a life of monotony, dissatisfaction, conformity, apathy and mediocrity, are:

   Excuse 1: **Wrong Timing:** 'Now is the wrong time.'

   Excuse 2: **External Circumstances and Commitments**: 'I need to do something for someone else.'

   Excuse 3: **Wrong Age:** 'I'm too old' or 'I'm too young.'

   Excuse 4: **Wrong Set of Skills, Upbringing or Experience**: 'I'm lucky to have a job right now. Period.'

   Excuse 5: **Don't Have The Money:** '…money is always an issue. If I win the lottery then…'

   Excuse 6: **Wrong Identity:** 'I'm not the successful type.'

   Excuse 7: **Wrong Place:** 'In my country, city or town all these ideas don't work.'
4. You need to revisit your professional direction. The world of work is changing and you must take the bull by the horns. Unemployment and redundancies are on the rise. Outsourcing, globalisation and the use of machinery at work are also increasing. Technology and the internet are changing the rules in the working environment. Generalised skills and retirement, in the way that you know them today, are under threat. The boundaries between life and work are narrowing, blurring boundaries and creating new health issues.
5. The **Corporate Escape Accelerated Programme: 7 Steps To Become A New Entrepreneur™** will give you a definite competitive advantage. As this popular quote says: 'Fail to plan, plan to fail.' The seven steps based on the acronym **COURAGE** are:

1. C is for Clarity. Know where you are and what you want. This is a strong foundation on which to build your future: your mission, your vision, your values and your life purpose.

2. O is for Opportunities and Obstacles. Here you will explore your skills, gifts, talents, strengths, knowledge, experience and also your weaknesses and potential areas for development.

3. U is for You: Unleash Your Potential. The aim here is to build your emotional resilience, expand your mind and shift your mindsets. When going from employee to becoming a New Entrepreneur your success depends greatly on this!

4. R is for Road Map. What exactly are you going to create and how are you going to make this happen? You will create a step-by-step action plan with milestones to measure your progress and success.

5. A is for Ask for Help and Support. What resources do you need? What skill set do you need to outsource? How can social media, partnership and joint ventures help you?

6. G is for Greater Good. What do you want to leave behind? What is going to be your legacy?

7. E is for Engage With Your Life. This step will help you create a lifestyle plan, where you make space for all eight of the main areas of your life, all working together and sustaining each other in harmony. Can you already imagine how different your life will be?

6. You can get started by taking your free **'Your Life Success Assessment: Discover The Naked Truth About 8 Key Areas Of Your Life'** www.maitebaron.com/lifesuccessassessment

> *"In times of change, those who are prepared to learn will inherit the land, while those who think they already know will find themselves wonderfully equipped to face a world that no longer exists."*
>
> Eric Hoffer

Conclusion

Congratulations On Reading This Book…

…you are now on the road towards taking control of your life and becoming a New Entrepreneur.

The book had some clear themes in it. For instance, you read about how you are born as a Leader and that it is only through socialisation, education and indoctrination that you become a follower. The good news is that now you also know this can be reversed at any time.

You also know something about how the status quo will do what it can to keep you small, because the little people who play the leadership game are scared of people who are able to think and stand up for themselves. Remember, the system is designed to control everything that matters: how you think, how you spend your money, what you do, how you live… so that power can be centralised and those in power can preserve their positions.

Your brain has an enormous plasticity and is well able to learn, to be stretched, challenged and expanded and it's your job to do this by learning how to master your mind so that you are in full control of your life.

Fear of change is only natural, especially as the system keeps trying to manipulate your emotions and mind as much as it can. So, always be selective about how you spend your time, the people you surround yourself with, the TV channels you watch, what you read, which films you chose to see. Everything matters, so stop feeding your mind with junk and instead look for quality not quantity. Become discerning, your mind is your best ally and it will help you achieve all you want in your life.

Remember these **5 Truths About Fear**™ to keep yours under control:

1. Fear is a friend in disguise and it visits everybody. The difference is how *you* deal with it.

2. Fear likes attention so it needs to be faced up to and challenged. The more you ignore it, the more it will bully you and the bigger it becomes.

3. Fear can't grow without you feeding it, so let it starve!

4. Fear checks your level of commitment towards something important you want or need.

5. Fear is an emotion of the future. If you keep living in the present, it can't appear.

To survive in today's changing world it's important to learn more than just new skills – you need to be able to make fundamental shifts in your attitudes, your beliefs and your paradigms to create the biggest difference in your life. It's the people who are responsive to change and flexible in their thinking who will continue to progress, while those who remain bound by habitual thinking will be permanently relegated to lower-grade jobs and earning the minimum wage.

Being able to challenge your own sense of identity requires courage, discipline and willpower and often, professional support as well, but I can guarantee that it's a worthwhile effort in the long run. After all, learning how to become agile in your approach to change is a long-term skill that will serve you well, whatever comes your way.

Remember, that if you never experience fear or excitement then you're almost certainly not learning anything. A reluctance to push through your fear means that you will remain bound by familiar habits, routines and paradigms, staying stuck and playing small.

Life is all about change. You just need to look at the seasons for evidence of this. Nature embraces change, yet people seldom do until it is forced upon them (and then they complain that no-one told them about it, despite the warning signs!).

What is happening now is less important than preparing yourself for the future. It's true, but most people don't understand this and struggle to live the life they want as a result. Many of you work hard to achieve a life of comfort and security but then proceed to stagnate as soon as you've done this, content to stay at your current level, neglecting the need to learn and grow.

There is no denying that change is difficult, so it's essential that you understand exactly why you need to do it if you're going to make things happen in your life. So, ask yourself what really drives you... and be honest! When things get tough (and they inevitably will), it's this drive that will keep you going.

It takes courage to live a meaningful life, so do not let others impose their values upon you. Be open and honest about your own values and what you truly want out of life and you will have no problem taking big steps towards your goals.

While you were reading the book, did you notice a recurring theme? Did you connect the dots in a way that make sense to you? When you do, you will discover that your past was perfect. It has equipped you to become the New Entrepreneur you were born to become, one who is open and able to seize all the opportunities that are there and open to you.

You may need to read this book again though, because it's not so much the content, but the story behind the content that matters. It's what comes next that really is important and which causes you to take action and implement all that you have learnt. But it's for you to decide to write the next chapter of your life, starting from today.

And always remember:

> *YOU are the director, the screenwriter and the star of your life-story. So make it a rich and exciting one! #CorporateEscape*

Afterword

Maite Barón's next book co-authored with Keith Grafton is called...

Branding The New Entrepreneur™: Rising From the Sea Of Sameness

Read on for a sneak peak:)...

Sneak Peak

Branding The New Entrepreneur™

Rising From the Sea Of Sameness

As a bonus for reading 'Corporate Escape: The Rise Of The New Entrepreneur', here's an excerpt from the new book:

We will take you on a journey that will help you create new foundations for your life so that all makes sense to you. We will help you see how that becoming a 'New Entrepreneur' is the future, *if* you want to be in charge of your life and your destiny.

But, in order to survive and thrive in this brave new world you need to rise from the millions of people who claim to be just like you and where, to all intents and purposes, you are just another fish in a 'sea of sameness'.

Branding The New Entrepreneur™ will show you how you can stand out from this crowd by discovering what is unique to you: your passion, your gifts, your true purpose, your voice and how you can bring your personality to make what you do stand out by bringing what's unique about you to the fore.

But best of all, by taking responsibility for your own life you will make the world a better place – the 'New Entrepreneur' cares about others and the legacy they leave behind.

In the meantime, if you are curious and want to start living the life you were born to live, I invite you to turn the pages and get started, let's begin this journey together.

Branding The New Entrepreneur™: Rising From the Sea Of Sameness is coming soon…

AFTERWORD

Action Page: 'To Do' and 'To Be' In The Next 30 Days

_____

_____

_____

_____

_____

_____

_____

_____

_____

_____

_____

_____

_____

_____

_____

So What's Next…?

Don't Forget To Get Your Bonuses ☑

Let's look at the two choices I offered you earlier: either do nothing and continue with your professional life as it is – although given current economic conditions this may not last for long – or take action and start living the life you've always dreamed of. I hope this book has inspired you to do the latter!

Next Steps→

If you haven't already, check out the bonuses and extra training materials I have put together for you; it's the best way I know to help you get started... after all, only new actions can create new results. Good luck!

* Book Reader's Resource Page → This is an exclusive page for all readers of the book where you can find exercises and activities to help you move forward. Everything we do is specifically developed for professionals who are faced with fundamental life changes and so it provides a new and fresh perspective on what your future could be like.

Get instant access at: **www.maitebaron.com/resourcepack**

* Free Training Webinars → Join a FREE 1 hour online training

We can support you as you identify and achieve your vision and goals both for today and into the future, helping you assess the options and opportunities available, and exploring how your existing skills and experience can help you shape a new life.

The webinar covers specific topics such as the mindset shifts that will help you in your transition from employment to self-employment, support you if you are between jobs or careers, and will enable you to take back control after redundancy and other setbacks.

Our webinars are a great opportunity for professionals on the move, those outside London, UK, or unable to attend our live workshops for any reason. You can attend our current webinars by registering at www.maitebaron.com/webinar

* **LIVE Events** → Generally these are one or two days workshops

After reading this book, you know that we help professionals, like you, who are at a crossroads in their lives, find new ways forward through a proven process. For some this professional transition is about escaping the frustrations of corporate life; for others who have been made redundant, or are in between jobs or careers, it is about discovering 'What next? and how to make it happen'. Our aim is to develop and support New Entrepreneurs from their early stages to achieve success on their terms.

Book your seat now at one of our FREE life-changing workshops, by going to: www.maitebaron.com/workshop

* **Communities** → Go to www.facebook.com/officialcorporateescape to join our community for real-time inspiration, updates, support and even more bonuses.

* **The 30-Week *Corporate Escape Accelerated Programme*: 7 Steps To Become A New Entrepreneur™** → Our flagship 30-week immersion programme is ideal for professionals looking to escape the rat race. It will help you through every stage of that transition, from getting clarity about what to do next through to creating a step-by-step action plan to escape, and then implementing it.

This Programme is part of **The Corporate Escape System™**: a process designed to support professionals, like you, through radical life changes, by helping you gain a new purpose and direction while leveraging your existing skills, knowledge and expertise so as to develop the business and marketing skills needed for you to thrive in today's changing world. These programmes will give you the breadth and depth of knowledge that you will need, these being by far the fastest and most intensive way I know to get you out of the corporate world and ready to achieve success and fulfillment on your terms.

There is a selection process for participants, as our aim is to deliver high quality programmes only to those professionals who are committed and willing to play an active part in achieving their own success.

You can apply by going to www.maitebaron.com/getstarted

About The Author

Maite Barón

PCC, MAC, ADVPAHyp, PATLT, NLPUTr, MANLP

Today Maite is 'The Corporate Escape Coach™' and a co-founder of **The Corporate Escape Foundation™**: 'Business with Heart & Soul' – a foundation born to bring passion and meaning back into the workplace and to leave a legacy behind of prosperity and purpose in society as a whole.

But this is not where it all started…

Maite Barón grew up in Barcelona and, having a passion for people and personal development, studied psychology, while working part-time in a fashion house. After two years, she left university disillusioned, believing that this was not the best way to help people in 'real time' in today's world.

Having started her career in high fashion, Maite worked in the industry for 14 further years as a freelance designer and forecaster for the likes of Balmain and Dior in both Barcelona and Paris, She eventually moved to work in London, only to be made redundant at 28. After this, she began a mail order catalogue business, a painful but also highly valuable business experience.

Returning to her love of helping others live their lives with passion, purpose and prosperity, Maite went on to teach interior design and become an artist in residence at the Kensington & Chelsea College. She then qualified in Neuro-Linguistic Programming (NLP), several other therapies, coaching and change processes while creating 'Positive Art' by commission for architects and private clients.

This period of intense learning and exploration filled the gap that psychology had failed to do, and she has worked in coaching, organisational development, consultancy and leadership development ever since. In this time, she has helped hundreds of professionals and executives gain clarity, focus and direction and overcome their fears and blockages so as to increase their performance during transition periods. She has worked both for private clients and organisations in a variety of industries, including Nestlé, Reuters and LG Electronics.

Though Maite is recognised and respected for her past corporate work in Europe and the UK, she believes that there is a need to bring the values, the heart and the soul back into the workplace. The easiest way to achieve this, she believes, is to create new businesses with different paradigms. So, her mission today has shifted towards helping those who are unhappy and disillusioned with corporate life to escape to become these 'New Entrepreneurs'.

Having lived in three countries, worked in five, changed career four times, been made redundant at 28, been married and divorced in the same year, and lost both of her parents within the space of just five years, Maite understands the stages and challenges that uncertainty, chaos and change bring to your life as a whole.

With her rich life experiences, as well as her wide-ranging professional expertise and qualifications, she is perfectly equipped to help you through any intense period of professional change in your life, whatever it may be.

Maite is well known for setting people free and leaving her clients feeling alive, in control of their lives, and excited about their futures.

The Corporate Escape Coach™

www.MaiteBaron.com

Lightning Source UK Ltd.
Milton Keynes UK
UKOW040636051012

200041UK00006BA/3/P